A Fresh Start FOR SINGLE PARENTS

Thomas Whiteman, Ph.D.
with Randy Petersen

SINGLES
Ministry Resources

David C. Cook Church Ministries
Colorado Springs, Colorado

A FRESH START FOR SINGLE PARENTS

Singles Ministry Resources Editorial Director: Jerry Jones
Cover Designer: Sonya Duckworth

Singles Ministry Resources
a division of Cook Communications Ministries
4050 Lee Vance View
Colorado Springs, CO 80918-7100
Cable address: DCCOOK

Printed in U. S. A.

Product code: 39511
ISBN: 0-7814-5384-4

The Fresh Start Single-Parenting Workbook is dedicated to all the single parents I have worked with over the past ten years while at Fresh Start. Not only have I had the privilege to minister to thousands of single parents, but also to minister together with a select few:

Nancy Ballein, Debbie Fleming, Sandi Harding, Tom Jones,
Karen King, Marilyn Rogers, Cheryl Smith, Bill Spicher

They have given me a glimpse of the day-to-day struggles, the exceptional courage, and the lack of support the average single parent must constantly endure. They have provided much of the inspiration for this book, as well as direct evidence that, with God's help, you can break the cycle of divorce and dysfunction with your children.

I must also acknowledge my wife,

Lori Whiteman

She has given me much of the material, as well as personal demonstrations of healthy parenting. It has been her dedication and efforts on behalf of my own children that have made me look like a good parent. Without her commitment to me and our children, this book would not have been possible.

Contents

Foreword by H. Norman Wright   *vi*
Introduction   *1*

1. The Plight of the Single Parent   *7*
2. Looking Back   *25*
3. Are We a Dysfunctional Family?   *51*
4. Breaking the Cycle   *73*
5. The Overburdened Parent   *99*
6. The Overburdened Child   *127*
7. Just for Dads   *151*
8. From Dating to Remarriage   *181*
9. Remarried . . . with Children   *215*

Appendix A: Action Points   *237*
Appendix B: Counseling References   *241*
Appendix C: Marriage and Divorce   *243*

Foreword

It's been my privilege to be acquainted with the written and spoken ministry of Tom Whiteman for several years.

In this practical resource, he once again gives evidence of his understanding and insight into the difficulties which single parents face today. With an interactional learning approach throughout, readers will end up having a better understanding of what has happened to them as well as having a clearer direction for their future. The feeling of being at the mercy of others and out of control should lift the further one moves into this volume. Readers should appreciate the balance between information and application that keeps this book moving along.

The author has clearly set out to answer the questions single parents are asking. All parents need help and support, and when traveling this road alone, the task is even more arduous. Fortunately, this book will make it easier and more livable.

H. Norman Wright
Director of Christian Marriage Enrichment;
Marriage, Family, and Child Counselor

Introduction

Cleaning out my attic last Saturday afternoon, I came across a box full of high school mementos. Of course, this made me stop my work while I perused its contents. My nostalgic stupor was interrupted by a letter that revived a disturbing memory. It was from a female friend I'd lost contact with after she dropped out of high school at age seventeen. It was rumored that she "had to get married." Her letter, which I had completely forgotten, confirmed the rumor and offered an explanation for her behavior. Let me share some of its contents with you.

Dear Tom,

   You must have passed out when you received this letter from me. Actually, I wanted to apologize to you for my sudden departure and the mystery about my absence. I guess you were shocked when you heard about my wedding.

   You see there was a lot going on in my life that I never told anyone. Last April my father told my mother that he didn't love her anymore. On Easter, he left and went to live with his secretary. I'd like to give opinions about her, but it's not my place to judge her. My mother was crushed. A few months before, mom had quit her job, so we had no income coming in. Pretty soon our credit cards ran out, and everyone seemed to be on our backs—the electric company, oil company, and the phone company. Well they threatened to take away the heat, electricity, and phone.

   My mom had all this on her shoulders as dad would not help. The phone was taken away, but the other bills we managed to pay and are still making back payments. First mom borrowed—because dad had taken all of the money out of the bank accounts—but how much can you borrow? So at age 18, Dave (older brother) became the best man I ever saw and went to work full-time; and he paid our mortgage, electricity, and oil bills. During this time our furnace and refrigerator broke down, and worst of all, my grandmother died.

I love Dave so much. If it weren't for him I think we would have died. Our family has become so close in the last year it's unbelievable.

Around the time that dad left I started going out with this guy, Steven. This is the same way my mom and dad met. They got together too fast and had to get married. Now I've done the same thing. Well you know the rest.

Please write back. This was a hard letter for me to write.

Love,
Nancy

Several times in the Old Testament, the Bible states that the iniquity of the fathers is visited on the children to the third and fourth generations (see Exod. 20:5, 34:7; Deut. 5:9). Nancy's letter testifies to the truth of that, as does most family research. But the Bible goes on to say that it doesn't have to be that way. With God's help, we can break the cycle of divorce and dysfunction with our children.

None of us want our "Daves" or our "Nancys" to have to experience the hardships of life that this letter has expressed. Yet in order to avoid the same mistakes, we will have to make some hard choices and do quite a bit of work. This workbook will help you identify some specific things that you can change about yourself and your parenting style that will have a lasting impact on you and your children.

What could be more difficult than trying to parent your children all by yourself? The noncustodial dad would probably respond, "Try not seeing your children for weeks at a time!" Most single parents would agree that this is not what they had in mind when they decided to have children (assuming that having children was even part of the plan).

I think we'd have to admit that there are no real winners in the battle for custody. And for both single moms and dads, life is a little more difficult and certainly more complicated than anticipated.

According to recent statistics, 40 percent of all children will spend some time in a single-parent family before their eighteenth birthday. This year, two million children will live with dad; fourteen million will live with mom. Divorce runs rampant, wreaking havoc in individual lives and families. Census figures from 1990 indicate that

B. MEN

> # Man at his best is R*esponsible*.

1. To his *work*. Gen. 2:15
2. To his *God*. Gen. 2:16-71
3. To his *family*. Gen. 2:24 *man leave father/ mother*

> Sin brings out the worst. Men have a deep craving for *significance* that he tries to fill without God.

1. We claim an identity in our *job*.
2. We claim meaning through *recreation*
3. When needed most, we *abadon ship*.

When Eve was being tempted

B. WOMEN

if left alone it gets worse

> # Woman at her best is R*elational*.

1. To her *kids*.
2. To her *my husband*.

> Sin brings out the worst. Women have a deep craving for *security* that she tries to fill without God.

1. If only I had a *baby*.
2. If only I had a *husband*.
   Before, unrealistic *expectations*
   After, unwarranted *bitterness*.

> To the woman's cry for security, fallen man responds with *distance or sex* *silent*

> To the man's cry for significance, fallen woman responds with *accusations*.

The path to wholeness begins with finding our *security* and *significance* in Christ.

and the rest falls into place

SURVEYING THE DAMAGE
Having Right Relationships #3
April 25, 1999

We learn much about relationships in the Garden of Eden.

1. WE ARE CREATED TO LIVE IN _relationship_ .

Long term _solitary confinement_ is considered inhumane.

2. MALES AND FEMALES ARE ~~Different~~ .

A. Different in _Creation_ . Gen. 2:7, 2:22   men - Dust woman - rib

B. Different in _form_ . Duh.

C. Different in _function_ . Gen. 2:18

3. B.F., INTIMACY WAS _normal_ .

Nakedness was not only a lack of _clothing_ but a _everywhere_ lack of _walls_ .
no barriers — oneness

4. THE ROOT CAUSE OF SIN IS OUR DESIRE TO LIVE
independently

5. SIN CREATED HAVOC IN OUR _relationships_ .

BETWEEN US AND GOD
Due to failing God, _shame_ .

BETWEEN ADAM AND EVE
Due to failing each other, _blame_ .

6. SIN BRINGS OUT THE _worst_ **IN ALL.**

▲. Creation

Before the Fall, _trees_ grew naturally. Gen. 2:9

After the Fall, _weeds/thorns_ grew naturally. Gen. 3:18

Jack pines   natural outcome   is bad

the fastest growing poverty group in our society is the single-parent family. Roughly 90 percent of the single moms make under $20,000 a year. (From "Living Alone and Loving It," *U.S. News and World Report*, August 3, 1987.) An ABC news special (11/21/91) stated that 23 percent make under $10,000. When you subtract the expense of day care, very little is left for living expenses.

The impact of divorce on children has been well documented in research. Economically, the U.S. Census Bureau has found that children can expect to become 37 percent poorer immediately after their parents' breakup. The book *Second Chances: Men, Women, and Children a Decade after Divorce* by Wallerstein and Blakeslee (1989) has become a watershed in material on the long-term emotional effects of growing up in a home where divorce has occurred. A review of this research and these manuscripts leads those of us in the helping professions to be discouraged or determined to try to make a difference. This book has grown out of my desire to make a difference.

Having conducted seminars around the country for the divorced, separated, widowed, and never married, and for single parents and their children, I have seen firsthand that there *is* hope. Single-parent families don't have to become part of the statistics but can actually break the cycle of divorce and dysfunction. But they need very practical help and direction, as well as divine intervention. That is the purpose of this book: to make a difference in the lives of single parents, by providing practical advice, guidance, and wisdom to those who are trying to parent alone.

HOW TO USE YOUR WORKBOOK

This workbook is designed for individual use, though it may be adapted for a small group. As an individual, work through it at your own pace. The sections "Make It Your Own" are for your use. Make it your own by adding extra information that you consider important; jotting questions to ask your counselor, pastor, or trusted friend; and making notes of therapeutic actions to undertake. Skip questions that don't apply to you, but don't dodge a question simply because it's difficult to answer.

The best way to work through this workbook is with someone else. If you can find another single parent who's willing to do this, arrange to work through a chapter (or part of a chapter) each week, then get together to talk about it. In this way, you can help each other sort through the issues raised and encourage each other to take specific steps to improve your situation.

It is possible to use this workbook in a small-group situation, meeting every week or every other week. However, some of the questions are quite personal. Small-group leaders will have to be sensitive to this and protect individual privacy while encouraging honesty.

There are many books on parenting, divorce, and widowhood. This book concentrates on the cycle of dysfunction and how to break it. It provides guidance on how to make the best of a bad situation—how to recognize the emotional problems of the single-parent home, and how to offer the love, support, and encouragement that overcomes them.

A WORD ABOUT STYLE

We have tried to make this book applicable to all single parents, custodial and noncustodial, mothers and fathers, divorced, widowed, and never married. However, the material is weighted somewhat toward custodial mothers who are divorced. Please make the necessary adaptations for your specific situation.

Right or wrong, most custodial parents are mothers (about 90 percent) and most noncustodial parents are the fathers. For convenience, whenever we refer to the custodial parent, we will address "Mom" and use the personal pronoun "she." We will address noncustodial references to "Dad" and "he." Suggestions for moms will usually assume that they have the children, and suggestions for dads will usually assume that they only see their children on weekends or less.

We often use examples from the lives of people we know. We have changed the names and some details to protect their privacy, but the impact of their stories remains true to life. Some of the material in this workbook is reprinted or adapted from other Fresh Start materials, especially *Innocent Victims* and *The Fresh Start Divorce Recovery Workbook*, both of which are published by Nelson. We hope the cartoons throughout the chapters will help you maintain your sense of humor as a single parent.

If you would like information about seminars or materials that Fresh Start offers, write or call our office.

FRESH START
63 Chestnut Road
Paoli, PA 19301

1-800-882-2799

The Plight of the Single Parent

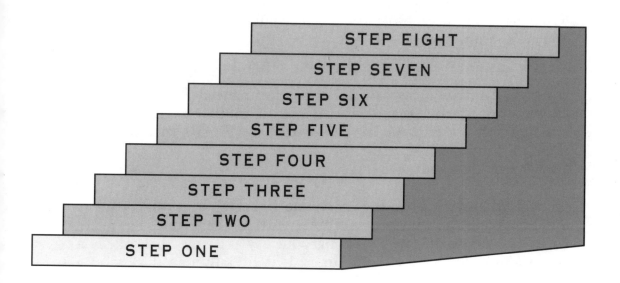

STEP ONE

Examine your attitude toward your situation.

"I will never forget those calm and cold words from my husband: 'Grow up, Scoti. I don't love you. I love Sandi. We are getting a divorce. You are so immature!'

"With those words ringing in my ears, I was catapulted on a painful journey down the lonely, dark road of single parenting. My marriage, my family, my beautiful home, my financial security—they're all gone. For nearly a year, I've been a single mother. I regret that my children will not grow up in the home of the parents that God gave them, but my husband made the choice to break his vow and chase after the myth of the greener grass.

"The pain never ends, though. Each day, I battle physical and mental exhaustion from the incredible financial stress, the pain of loneliness and the constant squabbles with my ex-spouse. How do I cope? Not very well. The old saying, 'One day at a time,' has taken on new significance for me. Sometimes, it is literally one minute at a time."

—A single mom with two young boys.
From "A Single Parent Shares the Pain"
Focus on the Family, January 1989

Handling the normal stresses and strains of life are difficult enough, but when you have to go it alone, your problems are compounded.

Another single parent put it this way:

"As a single parent of two preschool boys, I found my life going through an overwhelming set of changes. At first, I was too depressed to be of any good to anyone, including my boys. But as I moved along, I became determined that I was going to overcome my circumstances. That led me into my 'superwoman' role, where I tried to do everything by myself. I took a full-time job, arranged day care for the boys, ran the home, and tried to maintain a social life. I wanted to take the place of their missing father, but what I found was that I was becoming more and more frustrated, and the boys were usually mad at me. What a terrible feeling!

"Now I'm just trying to be a *decent* mother. I no longer need to be superwoman. I don't even have to be that good. I'm settling for doing the best I can and spending whatever time I can with the boys. It's like I wanted 100 percent before, and now I'm settling for 75 percent. But at least I might preserve my sanity this way, and who knows, maybe I'll even enjoy a few days."

—From *Innocent Victims*, by Thomas Whiteman

> Parenting as a single is an extremely challenging task. Your enjoyment of life depends on the attitude you have about your situation.

YOUR ATTITUDE TOWARD YOUR SITUATION

The apostle Paul said in the book of Philippians (4:11–13) that we need to learn to be content in whatever situation we find ourselves. That means that the key to our happiness as single parents is not in finding another spouse, or in obtaining financial security, or in any of those things; the key to our happiness lies in our learning to be content. That may take quite a bit of doing, especially if your marriage ended recently. In the immediate aftermath of a divorce—and perhaps for a year or two afterward—you will not feel content. You will feel stunned, angry, bitter, guilty, and depressed. But as you get back on your feet emotionally, make contentment one of your primary goals.

—— MAKE IT YOUR OWN ——

❶ Look through this list of adjectives, and circle the ones that describe how you feel about being a single parent.

resentful	excited	unsuccessful	encouraged
hopeless	independent	savvy	helpless
stretched	brave	needy	drained
focused	scattered	strong	lonely
wise	cheated	angry	courageous
content	hassled	inspired	pessimistic
grateful	bored	glad	guilty
bitter	calm	rushed	thankful

❷ Go back and look at the adjectives you circled. How many would you say are positive and how many negative?

Positive: _____

Negative: _____

❸ Now choose *one* of the negative emotions you circled. Choose one that you'd like to change. Write that emotion here: _____

❹ Write a sentence of 25 words or less that describes your current attitude (reflecting this emotion). Example: If I feel "cheated," I might say, "It's not fair that my spouse left to lead a carefree life while I'm stuck with the kids." Write your sentence here:

(1) _____

_____

Now notice the spaces below, numbered 2, 3, and 4. Leave 2 and 3 blank for now. In number 4, write *the statement you'd like to be able to say when you reach a point of contentment.* That is, I want to turn my feeling of being cheated into a feeling of contentment. I can't deny that bad things have happened to me, but I could say something like this: "My spouse wronged me, but my life has turned into something good as the kids and I have met new challenges." Write your own "contentment" sentence of 25 words or less in the #4 spot. Remember: This is not how you feel *right now*; you're merely imagining how you might express your contentment someday.

Peace is a process. Finding that contentment takes time. Imagine two points *along the way* to contentment, and put those feelings into words. For instance, my #2 statement might be, "It's not fair that my spouse left me, but at least I have the kids." My #3 statement might be, "My ex is free of the burden of childrearing but is missing out on its joys." See if you can fill in those spaces with "along the way" statements pertaining to the emotion you've listed.

(2) _____

_____

(3) _____

_____

(4) _____

_____

When do you think you might reach these points? Start by writing today's date in the margin beside statement #1. Then write the *projected* dates beside statements 2, 3, and 4. (NOTE: If you have just become a single parent, it may take a year or two to reach your desired point of contentment. If you have been dealing with this for a while, you may be ready to make these attitude changes in the next few weeks or months.)

> Your satisfaction with your life as a single parent is not based as much on your circumstances as it is on the attitude you choose toward your circumstances.

YOUR ATTITUDE AND YOUR CHILDREN

We've worked through just one of the negative emotions you listed. If you multiply that process by the number of negative feelings you listed, you might be overwhelmed. But contentment is contagious. As you make peace with certain emotions, that will overflow to others. There may be certain trouble spots—resentments or depressions you keep coming back to—but if you push forward in just one area, you will find your attitudes improving all along the line.

Your attitude influences your own enjoyment of life, as well as your children's adjustment. One of the most significant predictors of your children's success in life is your own adjustment as their parent.

It typically takes two years for a person to recover emotionally from a divorce or from a spouse's death.

Experts list five stages of grief that apply to divorce recovery as well as bereavement. The recovering person usually goes through denial, anger, bargaining, and depression, before finally reaching a point of acceptance.

You can't rush the process though you may want to. Once you understand the nature of the grieving process it will help you understand the feelings you're going through—including the feelings of your kids.

If you're still in the midst of recovery, you may need to consult other books (or counselors) to help you through that process. (One suggestion is *The Fresh Start Divorce Recovery Workbook* by Tom Whiteman & Bob Burns, which is available through the Fresh Start office at 1-800-882-2799 or most local bookstores.)

─────── **MAKE IT YOUR OWN** ───────

Before we move on to specific parenting issues, check your own recovery. These questions will serve as a health check. Unresolved issues will hamper your job of being a single parent until you can work through them.

❶ Are you over the denial phase, which means you accept the reality of the divorce and your responsibility to work on your own issues and your own recovery?   YES ＿＿＿   NO ＿＿＿

❷ Have you resolved the anger toward your ex-spouse, so that you no longer lash out at him or her, or stuff it inside, creating a turmoil of emotions that are just waiting to "get even"?   YES ＿＿＿   NO ＿＿＿

❸ Have you stopped trying to control or manipulate your former spouse into coming back or into being the type of parent you want them to be?   YES ＿＿＿   NO ＿＿＿

❹ Do you still suffer from guilt, not knowing how God views you as a divorced person?   YES ＿＿＿   NO ＿＿＿

❺ Have you worked through the depression that always affects us when we have experienced such a great loss in our lives?   YES ＿＿＿   NO ＿＿＿

❻ Have you reached a point of acceptance about the divorce, and are you determined to make the most of your life before God and before your children?   YES ____   NO ____

The success of your children's recovery from the trauma of divorce is in direct correlation with your own ability to heal and move on with your life. You can approach wholeness as a family by working toward wholeness yourself.

TWO ROADS

Obviously, your attitude about your present situation is closely tied to your attitude toward your former spouse, and how you interact with him or her. You can't do anything about how your former spouse treats your children, but you can work on how well *you* try to work with him or her. Let me illustrate this point by contrasting two real situations.

Nancy and Barbara are suburban housewives whose husbands left them for younger women as they were approaching their fortieth birthdays. Both had kids. Both were shocked and devastated. Each of them had only a high-school diploma, and neither had worked since getting married.

Nancy's Road

But that's where the similarities end. These two women have chosen different paths that reflect different attitudes. Nancy feels that life has victimized her. Every time she thinks of her ex, she grows angry and bitter. She takes pleasure in giving him a hard time. She got full legal and physical custody of their three children. She also won four years' worth of alimony, so that she could be trained for some new career.

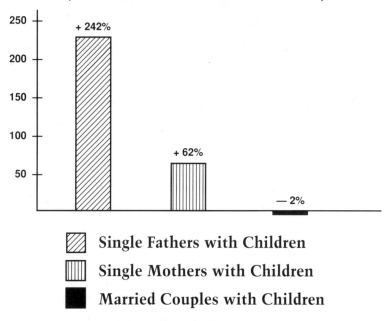

FIG. 1.1

THE CHANGING AMERICAN FAMILY

(PERCENT CHANGE FROM 1973 TO 1990)

Single Fathers with Children
Single Mothers with Children
Married Couples with Children

SOURCE: Knight-Ridder News Service

Three years after the divorce, Nancy works as a receptionist for little more than minimum wage. Whatever plans she had for training or a better job have gone by the wayside. "I'm really not very good at anything," she says. "Besides, I never wanted this divorce in the first place. I don't think I should have to work when I have three kids at home."

Nancy has distanced herself from most of her married friends, or maybe they're avoiding her. She feels more and more isolated, which increases her feelings of being victimized. Repeatedly she tells her children how unfair life has been. Her children feel sorry for her, but they've had a hard time too. They are poorer than before, and they miss their dad. When they want to visit him, they don't know how to tell their mom, because they feel guilty. He has not been a model father, missing alimony payments and putting off some visits, but in general he feels he has been there when they needed him. Their son, however, might disagree. He's been having problems in school and with social adjustment. He seems to be holding a lot of anger just under the surface.

Obviously, Nancy has never forgiven her husband for the divorce. She bristles a bit at the "polite" way they treat each other when dealing with the kids. "He expects me to act as if nothing's wrong. Well something *is* wrong, and I'm not going to forget it."

Barbara's Road

Barbara is a different story. She went back to school and headed toward a business administration degree. She is now doing word processing out of her home and has some good prospects for full-time employment. She arranged to share legal custody of the children with her ex-husband, but she retained physical custody. In this way, she hopes that her husband will be more involved in the children's lives. "I may not be married to him," she says, "but he is still their father. Even though he didn't turn out to be such a good husband, he was always a good father, and I believe he still is."

The children enjoy their visits with their father. They don't hesitate to tell mom all about their weekends away, because they know she is genuinely interested in their relationship with him.

Barbara has found a new group of friends who have been through similar life changes. Yet she remains friendly with one or two of the married couples she knew before. She has described her life in this way: "I wouldn't wish divorce on my worst enemy, but I wouldn't trade anything for what I have learned having gone through a divorce. I have more self-confidence and feel more fulfilled now than ever before, because I'm no longer dependent on my husband. Sure I get lonely sometimes, but there are worse things than being single and lonely, and one of them is to be in a bad marriage. Besides, now I have much stronger friendships and a closer relationship with my kids."

Barbara's children, after a period of adjustment, are now doing better than ever in school and with their friends. They seem to be adjusting to the single-parent situation quite well.

----- MAKE IT YOUR OWN -----

❶ Which single mom's story sounded most like your own situation?

_____

❷ To what do you attribute Barbara's success as a single parent? Check the one that you believe was most influential:

- ☐ a. She's one in a million and should consider herself lucky.
- ☐ b. Going back to school is what really helped her the most.
- ☐ c. She probably has a more reasonable ex-husband.
- ☐ d. Her children are exceptionally compliant.
- ☐ e. She has taken full responsibility for her own life, and is working with her ex for the good of her children.
- ☐ f. This example is a figment of the author's imagination, and doesn't happen in real life.

What's the "right" answer? Your answer reveals a lot about you. If you picked *a.* or *f.*, you are probably still angry with your ex, or you are depressed about your situation and unable to imagine anything good coming out of the experience.

If you picked *b., c.,* or *d.,* you are probably choosing from your own experience. You may be frustrated at your lack of education, or you may be having difficulty with your ex-spouse or kids. And you are probably right. Barbara seems blessed in all these areas. However, I believe the most helpful characteristic found in Barbara's situation is in her attitude (*e*).

The greatest miracle that God works is in transforming *you*. God can empower you to change your situation.

❸ What would it take to make your situation more like Barbara's?

- ☐ Going back to school.
- ☐ Finding a better job.
- ☐ Forging a truce with my ex.
- ☐ Giving the kids something more than a talk, but I'm not sure what.

☐ Pretending that everything's okay.

☐ Experiencing an act of God.

☐ Other _____

> A good attitude faces up to a difficult situation and takes responsibility for changing it.

LEMONADE, ANYONE?

Most single parents are single parents because of some sort of tragedy. Most, of course, are divorced. The divorce itself, along with the infidelity or abuse that may have led to it, is very painful. And in most cases (though not all), it is the custodial parent who has suffered the most.

Other single parents have been widowed. The death of a spouse is the greatest emotional upheaval most of us will ever face. There is great sadness, pain, and depression. And there is often anger at God—especially since, in most single-parent cases, the spouse has been taken away while still relatively young. This seems unfair. The divorced person can turn anger toward the ex-spouse; the widowed can only rail at God (or whatever forces caused the death).

For still other single mothers, the pregnancy itself was an emotional jolt. You may feel noble for not choosing abortion, but then your whole life changes. In the film *Baby Boom*, the single mom played by Diane Keaton tries to continue her business career but finds that she just can't do it all. Frustration and anger are often the results in such a situation.

It just seems as if bad attitudes go along with single parenting. Bad things have happened. Life is tough. How are you going to get through?

One of my favorite posters features a man with a funnel in his head and a spigot where his nose should be. In the funnel is a bunch of lemons and, out of the spigot, lemonade is pouring into a pitcher. The caption reads, "When life gives you lemons, make lemonade."

This is the difference between Nancy and Barbara. Both got lemons; only Barbara turned them into something tasty.

We have all been given some lemons in our lives. (Some of us married them.) Yet, in spite of those bitter experiences, we still have the ability to choose our own attitude toward our circumstances. Will we choose to become bitter, to squeeze those lemons and serve other people lemon juice? You know what happens when someone serves lemon juice. The sour taste turns people away. We alienate our friends, our children, and ourselves.

Or will we choose to add some sugar to that lemon juice and serve lemonade? The sugar that we all possess is our positive disposition: the ability to forgive, to love, and to uplift others. When we add this to the bitter experiences of life, we find a perfect combination of sweet and sour, which attracts others as lemonade does on a hot day.

For you, the question remains, "What will my attitude be toward my circumstances?" Will it be bitterness, self-pity, and immobilization, as in Nancy's story? Or will you choose forgiveness, hope, endurance, and determination, as Barbara did?

Now I know you're thinking, "Yeah but you don't understand how much I've been hurt." Or "You can't imagine what a creep I was married to." Maybe you are right. Your circumstances may be terrible. But how are you going to choose to respond? Are you going to be a victim or a victor? And before you answer that you'd rather remain in your self-pity, think about your children. Do you want them to overcome their circumstances? What attitude would you like for them to choose? Remember that your attitude is the biggest predictor of your child's adjustment.

You can serve lemon juice to your kids and to everyone else. Or you can serve lemonade. It's your choice!

SPOTLIGHT: JOSEPH

The Book of Genesis tells the story of Joseph who turned huge negatives into great positives. He was sold into slavery by his brothers, but he worked so well that he became head of his master's household.

Joseph was falsely accused of rape by his master's wife and thrown into prison. Even in an Egyptian prison, he won favor. When the king had a troubling dream, a former prisoner remembered that Joseph had a knack for interpreting dreams. When summoned, Joseph revealed the meaning of the king's dream and was made second-in-command in Egypt.

When famine hit, Joseph was in charge of food distribution. His brothers came to Egypt to beg for food. Joseph had the power to kill the ones who had gotten him into all those messes, but eventually he revealed himself to them and welcomed them happily.

"You meant evil when you did this to me," he told his brothers. "But God meant it for good."

Throughout his life, Joseph maintained a forgiving spirit, an attitude that rolled with the punches and won out.

Joseph's story may seem long ago and far away. But I wish you could meet Darla, a friend of mine with a story that may be similar to yours. Her husband left her with two young children nine years ago. Over the years she has sought reconciliation, and he has returned—only to leave again, and again. She has weathered disappointment after disappointment, but with God's help she has maintained a spirit free from bitterness.

"I'd be crazy if I didn't have the attitude that I have," she says. "I know in my heart that God is working things out for my good. I also think of that verse where Joseph says, 'You meant it for evil, but God meant it for good.'"

That's no pie-in-the-sky optimism. It's a deep faith forged by years of emotional suffering. It's a lesson we all need to learn.

———— MAKE IT YOUR OWN ————

❶ How do you respond to the Joseph story?

- ☐ It's a nice story, but life isn't like that.
- ☐ That may work for brilliant, holy people, but not for me.
- ☐ It's an inspiration, but I'm not there yet.
- ☐ I've seen a few cases where evil intentions were turned to good things.
- ☐ God is the source of my problems! How can I expect him to remove them?

□ Other _____

_____

_____

❷ Whom (if anyone) do you blame most for your situation?

_____

❸ What is the first step you could take toward forgiving this person (even if it's yourself or God)?

SINGLE PARENT FACT SHEET

1. There are 16 million children in single-parent homes; 14 million live with mother, and 2 million live with father.

2. One half of all single mothers receive no child support. Half of the children involved do not see their fathers on a regular basis two years beyond the breakup of the family.

3. The majority of single parents are between the ages of 27 and 34. Single parents over 40 are increasing in numbers due to the trend by many women to delay childbearing.

4. More and more professional women are choosing to have children on their own due to the "ticking biological time clock" and because of the unavailability of a healthy male relationship.

5. Single moms spend less time looking for a man than they do trying to find child care, medical insurance, emotional support, and ways to save money.

6. Today's single parent is generally a nurturing, resourceful parent who works hard and is responsible and conscientious. She or he is an informed consumer and a buyer of all kinds of products.

4 In what ways can you imagine these painful events being turned into something good? How?

Action Point: Perhaps this question of forgiveness has uncovered a relationship that needs some work. If so, write the name of this person here and on page 237 (appendix A). (Appendix A will list all of the Action Points for later reference and for an overview of your short and long term goals.)

If the baggage of your divorce or your spouse's death is still holding you back, take the time to consult a counselor or to read one of the many helpful divorce recovery or grief recovery books available. (See appendix B for a list of recommended resources.)

> Every journey starts with a single step. And it continues with a series of single steps.

You don't recover from a divorce overnight, but you can take a step. For many people, recovery starts with a simple *decision* to recover. They figure out what *they* are going to do to start living again. That's the attitude you need to begin your journey toward wholeness.

─────── **MAKE IT YOUR OWN** ───────

1 From these facts, how "average" are you?

☐ I'm a single mom.

☐ I'm a single dad.

☐ I receive no child support.

☐ My children do not see their father.

☐ I am between the ages of 27 and 34.

☐ I would rather raise my children on my own than accept a relationship with a man that is less than healthy.

- [ ] I spend more time taking care of my children's needs than on my own social needs.
- [ ] I am a good, resourceful parent.
- [ ] I'm a smart consumer.

Looking Back

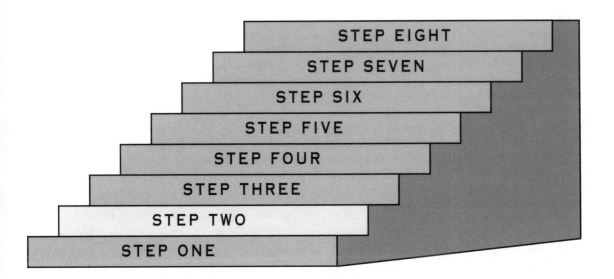

STEP TWO

*Make sure you have resolved the issues
from the past relationship for
you and your children.*

Bobby was sound asleep when his mother shook him to get him up. "Get up, Bobby! Grab your blankie and teddy bear. We're going bye-bye."

Bobby, who was only five-and-a-half years old, quickly grabbed his things as his mother whisked him away in the middle of the night. He remembered very little beyond that point as he drifted in and out of sleep. His mother took him downstairs, loaded him into a car full of family belongings and drove to Bobby's grandmother's house at the other end of town.

When Bobby woke up the following morning and saw that he was at his grandmother's, he realized that he hadn't been dreaming about the night before. He was glad to be at his grandmom's but was a little confused as to why they left home so abruptly.

Bobby asked his mother lots of questions as they sat around the breakfast table. "Where is Daddy? What are we going to do today? And when are we going home?"

Do you remember that fateful day when you first became a single parent? The end of a committed relationship has a big impact on the entire family.

———— MAKE IT YOUR OWN ————

❶ What do you recall about the day you became a single parent? What events come to mind? _____

_____

_____

❷ What were your feelings at that time? _____

_____

_____

❸ How did your children react? _____

_____

_____

We are going to look back. You may find ways to correct any mistakes you've made. It is not too late to find out how best to work through the issues with your children.

BREAKING THE NEWS TO YOUR CHILDREN

The book of Ephesians says that we are to "speak the truth in love." This type of communication should take place among all parties involved in a separation or divorce. This guideline affects the answers to some of the most commonly asked questions about children and divorce.

❶ What does "speaking the truth in love" mean to you? _____

_____

_____

❷ Check those to whom you spoke the truth in love in your present situation:

- ☐ spouse
- ☐ children
- ☐ parents
- ☐ friends

❸ How did you experience God's support during this sharing? _____

_____

_____

_____

_____

When should you start to prepare your children for a divorce?
Prepare your children as soon as the possibility of divorce is apparent.
Kids usually know that "there is something going on" long before you
credit them for knowing.

For marital problems, get help but don't feel compelled to tell the
children anything of a personal nature between you and your spouse. If
the children ask, use this opportunity to demonstrate the proper way
to handle problems. "Your mother and I are having some personal
problems that we need to work out. Because we are committed to each
other and to the family, we want to get help in resolving these problems as quickly as we can."

Once the problem reaches a point where divorce or separation is
apparent, then it affects the whole family. The children need to be told
as soon as it can be arranged. Only delay this matter if you need to
work out some details, or if it falls on an important day such as
Christmas or one of the children's birthdays. It is reasonable to wait
until some of the details are worked out, such as: Where will mom
live? Where will dad live? Where will the kids stay? How often will we
see each parent? If these matters cannot be settled, sit down with
them and tell them as much as you know.

Many parents tend to "protect" their children from the truth as
long as possible. One study found that 80 percent of the preschoolers
questioned had received no information about their parents' separation. Parents do a disservice to the child by withholding such information. Withholding creates anxiety about the future and distrust toward
the parents.

———— MAKE IT YOUR OWN ————

❶ *When* did you break the news?
  ☐ When we first began to have trouble.
  ☐ When we knew there was no hope of reconciliation.

☐ When one spouse moved out.

☐ When the divorce was final.

☐ Other. _____

_____

❷ Do you feel this timing was

    ☐ Too soon

    ☐ Too late

    ☐ About right

If possible, both parents should sit down with the kids and tell them about the separation or divorce together, before one of the parents leaves. If the separation happens abruptly, the parent with the children will need to give them some preliminary information right away, but as soon as it can be arranged, both parents need to come together to tell the children what will happen to the family. This method is important for several reasons:

▶ Having both parents present offers the greatest possibility of a balanced and honest presentation.

▶ If the children have any questions, they can address them to the parent who is best able to answer.

▶ The "united front" makes it clear that both parents are in agreement on the decision. This helps to reduce the splitting of loyalties, the playing of one parent against the other, and the fantasy that "my parents will work this out." If one parent is missing, the children are likely to think, "Yeah, that's what mom says, but dad probably disagrees."

If one parent is not present, then it is even more important that the parent who tells the children remembers to speak the truth as lovingly as possible. Representing both sides of the issue is difficult when you are so emotionally involved. Let the children know that it is an issue between their parents and that you both still love them.

Try to answer questions about the other parent as honestly as possible. State what you know to be true, as nicely as you can.

❶ *How* did you tell the kids? (Check all that apply.)
- ☐ Together
- ☐ Alone
- ☐ Both separately
- ☐ Respectfully of other parent
- ☐ Bad-mouthing other parent
- ☐ Reassuring
- ☐ Clearly and directly
- ☐ Sort of hinted at it
- ☐ Repeatedly
- ☐ Once, and never talked about it again
- ☐ Other. _____

_____

❷ If you could do it over again, what would you do differently? _____

_____

_____

❸ *How difficult* was it to tell your kids about the breakup?
- ☐ Extremely difficult
- ☐ Harder than I expected
- ☐ Easier than I expected
- ☐ Not so hard
- ☐ Other. _____

_____

❹ What was the hardest thing about it?
- ☐ Being fair to the other parent
- ☐ Not falling apart myself
- ☐ Reassuring my child when I was worried about the future

☐ Feeling guilt about the situation
☐ Worrying about how my kid would take it
☐ Other. _____

How much should we tell the children? When deciding how much to tell the kids, take into consideration your child's developmental level.

If children know enough to ask the questions, then they're old enough to get honest answers.

The key points to cover include these:

▶ How did this happen? What are the reasons?

▶ Do you still love me? Does my mother/father still love me? Am I wanted?

▶ How will my life change? Where will I live, go to school, church?

▶ Am I part of the reason for the breakup? Could I have done something to avoid this separation/divorce?

Discuss what will happen to the children. Reassure them of your love for them, and be prepared to back it up with actions. Give the child permission to love _both_ parents. For preschoolers it is important to reassure them that they will be cared for, and then explain the divorce in terms they can understand.

Children who are elementary age or older need more specific information, particularly about where they will live and the visitation arrangements. They will also require more specific information about what went wrong.

Don't expect your children to understand your explanations or to ask all of their questions the first time you talk about it. Be prepared to explain the situation and answer questions over and over again. Stress that separation and/or divorce is an adult decision. It was not their fault, nor can they do anything to get the parents back together.

What if the truth is particularly "ugly" or hard to talk about? It is easier to deal with what we know far better than what we imagine. Tell them the truth in as loving a way as you can. The earlier they hear the truth, the sooner they can start to deal with the problem and begin the healing process. You need to use discretion regarding the age of the children and how much they really can understand. But once again, if they are old enough to ask the question, they are old enough to hear an honest answer. For example, if Dad is leaving because he has a girlfriend, you may not want to give them this information in the first meeting. Soon thereafter, however, you need to tell them what is really going on. Sooner or later, the kids hear the whispers and innuendos, so it is best that they hear it in a straightforward manner from their parents. In a case like that, if possible, the information should come from *Dad*. That way the children know that they are hearing firsthand information, which is usually more reliable. They then have an opportunity to openly discuss their questions and concerns.

The father in this case should examine his motives before the talk, however. As one father said, "The difficulty in being totally honest with your children is that you have to decide whether it's something you're doing for your own benefit or whether it's something that's going to benefit them."

If Dad is not available, or not willing to talk with the children, then it obviously falls on the other parent to present as balanced an explanation as possible. Then, if the children have questions, you may want to offer to let them discuss the issue with someone a little more neutral. This might be an aunt or uncle they trust, a counselor at school or church, or a relative on their father's side, whom they might view as being more objective. Your children may not want to do this, but it is important that you at least offer. This allows them the opportunity to seek a "second opinion" without feeling that they are betraying you.

This open communication is one of the key elements in a healthy family. Dysfunctional families are marked by too much interaction, known as enmeshment, too little communication or emotional distancing, and distorted messages, as found in controlling and manipulative families. Healthy interactions allow for open discussion and honest questioning and invite verification.

——— MAKE IT YOUR OWN ———

❶ Which of the following points do you feel you covered satisfactorily?

- ☐ How did this happen? What are the reasons?
- ☐ Do you still love me? Does mother/father still love me?
- ☐ Am I wanted?
- ☐ How will my life change? Where will I live, go to school, church, etc.?
- ☐ Am I part of the reason for the breakup? Could I have done something to avoid this separation/divorce?

❷ Is there something else you wish you had said when you first talked with your children about this? _____

_____

_____

> Tell your children the truth in as loving a way
> as possible.

What about the cases where the child is abandoned by one of the parents? When someone apparently abandons his or her children, it is difficult to speak the truth in a loving way. You rarely know what the truth is. In cases of abandonment, the remaining parent needs to balance the comments so that the children do not have undue hope *or* despair. Do reassure the child of his or her lovability.

Aren't children really tougher than we think? Yes. They can eventually recover, no matter how difficult the truth is to hear. Most children can handle reality when their parents take time to communicate honestly with them. That does not mean we must "tell all" to the kids. They will bounce back from the basics, difficult as they are, but they don't need to be overwhelmed with the play-by-play. *Details are seldom necessary, but honesty is critical.*

How can I expect my children to react when we give them the news? Your child's reaction will vary according to his or her developmental level and personality, but generally you can expect some of the following reactions:

▶ *Underreaction.* This may be a form of denial and the beginning of the grieving process. Don't be surprised when your child reacts with, "Can I go out and play now?" Some parents are happily surprised at this: "Brenda seems to be dealing very nicely with our divorce." Only years later the buried feelings emerge in a much more dangerous way. At some point, when your child is ready, you may need to urge him or her to "let it all out," to express all the rage or sadness or fear that he or she feels. This may be painful for you, but it is important for the child to have opportunities to express feelings, even years after the events.

▶ *Preoccupation with egocentric thoughts.* In certain developmental stages, children cannot help but react in self-centered ways. Your child may react with, "What about my birthday?"; or, "Who's going to take me to Disney World?" These are merely concrete expressions of fear for the future. Your child needs reassurance of how he or she fits into your new life.

▶ *Lack of interest in the details of the breakup.* This reaction may reflect the child's inability to comprehend the news and the fear of talking about it. They may have no questions. Keep the lines of communication open. After your initial discussion, create ongoing opportunities for the children to express their concerns.

▶ *Strong, hysterical reaction.* It is possible for a child to respond with rage and flagrant misbehavior. The rage is a natural emotional reaction and the misbehavior is probably an attempt to manipulate the parents' decisions or at least to register a protest.

It takes courage on the part of the parents to understand the children's feelings and allow the children to express their pain. This will accelerate acceptance and growth on the part of the child.

—————— **MAKE IT YOUR OWN** ——————

❶ How did your children *react*? (Check all that apply.)
  ☐ Underreaction
  ☐ Self-centered
  ☐ Lack of interest in details of the breakup
  ☐ Rage, hysteria
  ☐ Misbehavior
  ☐ Withdrawn
  ☐ They don't trust me any more
  ☐ Very well, actually. We've grown closer
  ☐ Other. _____
  _____

❷ What kind of reaction did you expect? _____
  _____

❸ How did you handle your children's reaction? _____
  _____
  _____

—————— **MAKE IT YOUR OWN** ——————

As you look back, it's easy to see all the wrong things you did. It is a difficult task. Do you understand some things more clearly now? As time brings healing, can you "speak the truth" more lovingly?

Why not use this page to practice? Write a letter to your child(ren). I'll start it for you—it's up to you to finish and deliver it.

Dear _____,

I never told you this in the right way, because I wasn't sure how. But it's important for you to know. So I'm going to try.

_____

_____

_____

_____

_____

BREAKING THE NEWS
TO YOUR CHILDREN

1. Be honest and open in the way you present the information. Give explanations, not defenses or opinions.

2. Focus on what will happen to each child. Assure them of their continued well-being, in spite of difficult transitions.

3. Make sure the children understand that they were not the cause of the divorce.

4. Give clear and definite statements of mutual love and acceptance. Be prepared to back this up with actions such as hugs, interest in their world, and a listening ear.

5. Let them know that they can't get their parents back together. Encourage a realistic view of what life will be like after the divorce.

6. Expect that you will have to reinforce this information by opening discussions with your children about the divorce at regular intervals throughout their lives.

Action Point: Choose a time and place where you can begin to give your children this message. Write it here in the form of a goal, and in Appendix A, which will list all your Action Points. _____

_____

_____

YOUR CHILD'S REACTION:
THE FIRST COUPLE OF YEARS

Children go through the same basic stages of grieving as adults. Anytime there is a loss of a significant relationship, either through death or divorce, we go through a process of grieving. This process usually lasts for at least two years and is distinguished by specific emotional stages.

The Initial Stage

In the first six months to a year, children typically experience *denial* and *anger*. Denial is a normal way our minds deal with painful information.

Children may encounter news of a divorce (or death) by denying the fact itself ("Daddy's just away on a trip"); denying its irreversibility ("They'll get back together eventually"); or denying the seriousness of it ("My life won't really change much"). In their own time, they will need to come to grips with each of these things.

Preschool children are usually too young to understand fully what's going on. They come by denial naturally. At a later time, they may begin the grieving process—perhaps as they begin school and realize that other families have two parents.

School-age children (6–12) will often express denial by pretending nothing has happened. They may go about their normal activities and perhaps even improve their behavior (as they recognize that Mom or Dad is hurting).

Teenagers often deny by escaping. They will spend more time away from home, immersing themselves in activities at school or with friends. Home reminds them of what they've lost, and they don't want to deal with that.

You can do little about denial. Be honest about the situation and your feelings.

Anger is the natural response when denial wears out. Picture a

FIG. 2.1
PHASE ONE: INITIAL REACTIONS

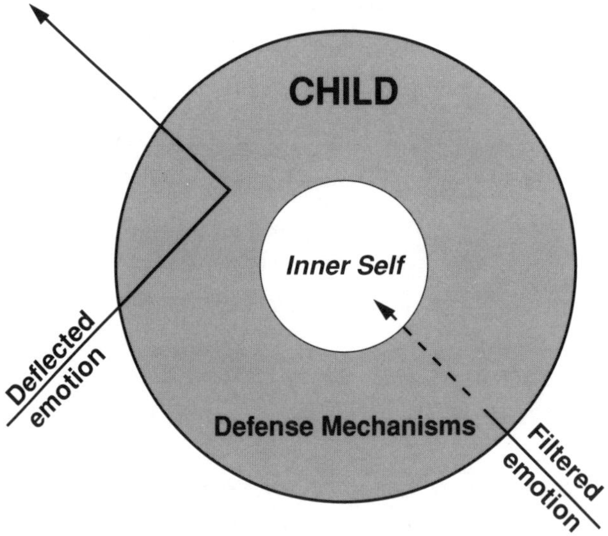

Defense Mechanisms — Denial and Anger

person as a circle. We all put up defense mechanisms, especially when we're in crisis. Picture this as an outer circle around our core selves. In denial, painful realities are deflected by this shield. We just don't let them in. But eventually the shield wears down. Reality penetrates, and it hurts! We act like emotional cyclotrons, spinning those feelings and flinging them out in anger at anyone around us.

Especially with younger kids, anger is often misdirected. They can lash out at friends, school authorities, or themselves, when really they are mad at you and their other parent (for splitting up) or at God (for letting it happen).

How can you deal with this? Try to focus their anger. Give them permission to be mad at you (or at the other parent or at God), and try to help them forgive. Accept their anger toward the other parent, and help them deal positively with it.

Older children can be much more specific, as they develop their critical abilities. They choose the targets of their anger more carefully. They will decide *which* parent is to blame and what the causes were.

Anger is never an excuse for inappropriate behavior. Teach your kids that they must pay the price for misbehaving. They must be responsible for their actions, even if they were angry.

Be cautious about anger that your children direct toward themselves. Watch for a preoccupation with guilt or self-destructive behavior. Talk openly and repeatedly about these issues. Your children must know that they are not to blame.

The Secondary Stage

Eventually, children realize that anger doesn't work. They try to turn those negative feelings into positive actions. "Maybe I can save the situation yet. Maybe I can solve the problems."

We call this next step "bargaining." Children will commit themselves to all sorts of positive actions, hoping to avert the problems. It seldom works.

In this stage, the painful realities are beginning to hit home, but there's one last shield of determination that bounces them back. Bargainers attempt simple solutions to complex problems and usually fail.

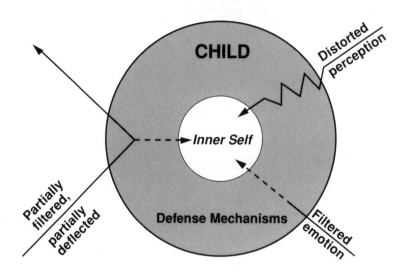

FIG. 2.2

PHASE TWO: SECONDARY REACTIONS

Defense Mechanisms — Bargaining and Depression

In the movie *Paradise*, the divorcing parents, played by Don Johnson and Melanie Griffith, are brought back together by their enterprising child. This is a classic bargaining fantasy. It is fun to watch because we want this to happen. But the truth is that children's attempts to manipulate their parents' decisions usually hurt more than help.

When a child realizes that there's little he or she can do to fix things, depression sets in. This can come in the form of withdrawal or escape. It can involve sadness, confusion, listlessness, anxiety, and a host of physical symptoms. Very young children tend to be clingy or fearful and generally uncooperative. Older kids become ornery or rebellious.

While bargaining deflects the painful realities of the divorce; depression *distorts* the realities. They view the death or divorce through distorting glasses that can make the situation seem worse than it is or place blame where it doesn't belong.

40 *SINGLE-PARENTING WORKBOOK*

Depression is basically a shutdown of emotions. Painful reality has finally penetrated to the core of one's being, and it hurts like crazy. What's the use of going on?

> Pain is a necessary part of the healing process for your children. Only after depression can they reach acceptance.

How to help your children through the pain:

▶ Encourage your children to talk about their feelings. Don't trivialize their feelings or make light of their loss. Don't assume that you

FIG. 2.3
PHASE THREE: ACCEPTANCE

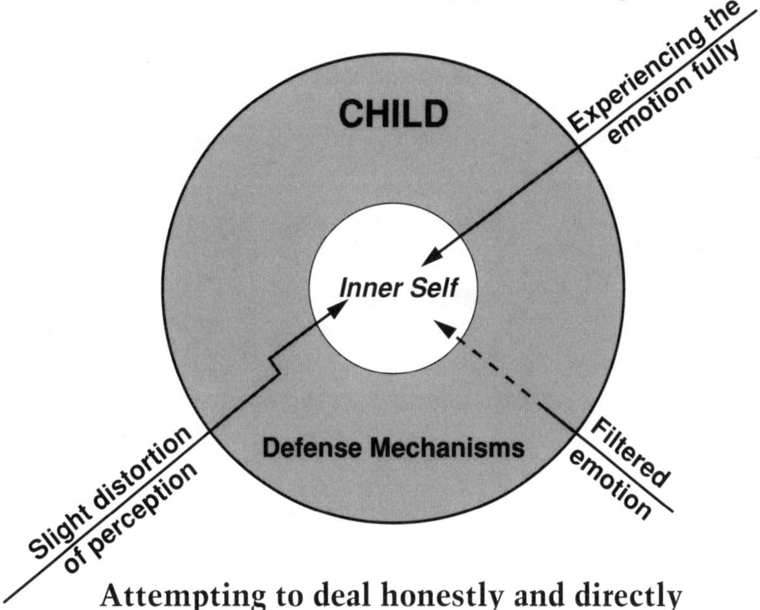

CHILD

Experiencing the emotion fully

Inner Self

Slight distortion of perception

Defense Mechanisms

Filtered emotion

Attempting to deal honestly and directly with our situation

know exactly how they feel or that you have shared all those feelings. Allow them to express their unique pain.

▶ Be honest. Don't hold out hope of a resolution that doesn't exist.

▶ Be honest about your own feelings but don't go to pieces. If you are able to express feelings without being incapacitated by them, your children may follow suit.

▶ Find some healthy activities for your children, something new and exciting.

Acceptance: The Final Stage

Depression goes away, if you give it time. The wounds heal.

Children regain self-confidence. They learn to forgive. They build new relationships and patch up old ones. They take risks again and accept responsibility. If depression persists for more than two years after "impact," seek professional help.

Following a significant loss from death or divorce, children need to go through the normal stages of grieving, which can take at least two years.

When we reach a point of acceptance, we are able to deal with the world around us in healthy ways. We accept the full impact of the divorce with little or no distortion. We have accepted the pain and changes in our lives, and we are now free to move forward with our lives. We are willing to risk again.

Here is a time line, showing a typical recovery process. Over a two-year period, the person moves through denial, anger, bargaining, depression, and rather suddenly to acceptance.

Fig. 2.4

CRISIS TIME LINE
(THE SLIPPERY SLOPE)

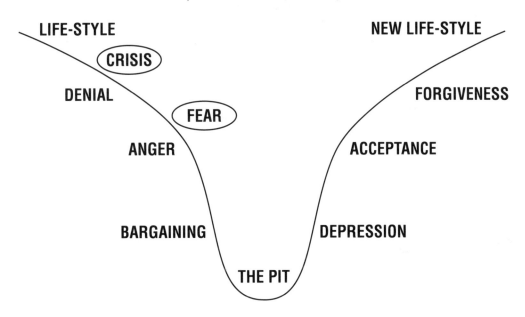

Now here's your time line. How would you draw *your* recovery? The crisis is the impact—when you first dealt with the shock of divorce, separation, impending divorce, spouse's death, or terminal illness. The graph covers approximately a two-year period. But if your recovery has lasted longer, this could be a four-year period.

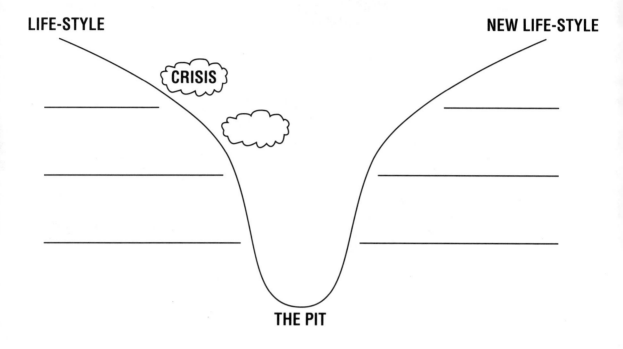

FIG. 2.5

CRISIS TIME LINE

LIFE-STYLE

CRISIS

NEW LIFE-STYLE

THE PIT

❶ In what stage do you find yourself? _____

❷ What three things might you do to speed your "recovery"?

    1. _____

    2. _____

    3. _____

Now chart your kids' progress, as much as you can, on the graph you used for yourself. (If you have more than one child, use colored pens to graph each child.) Diagram their recovery in the same way.

Now fill out the chart for each of your children.

	CHILD #1	CHILD #2	CHILD #3
Present Stage			
Symptoms			
What I'm doing about it			

As you look over the graphs and the chart, look for any indication that your child is "stuck" in one area. You may need to take some special action (a talk, a new activity, discipline) to get your child "unstuck."

Action Point: On the basis of the section you've just read, what course of action will you follow to help your child(ren) through the recovery process? _____

_____

_____

_____

Write this goal again in Appendix A as one of your "Action Points."

THE EFFECTS OF DIVORCE ON CHILDREN: THE LONGER TERM

A number of studies have demonstrated that children react to their parents' divorce well after the initial stages of grieving. These reactions fall into three general categories.

The first category, which includes approximately one-quarter (about 28 percent) of the children of divorce, contains those children who come through their parents' breakup in a fairly healthy manner. They go through the normal grieving process, experiencing denial, anger, bargaining, and depression, and (usually within two years) reach a point of acceptance. This acceptance seems contingent upon their parents' ability to work through an amicable settlement. This acceptance usually includes a reduced number of disruptions following the divorce, such as remarriage, a major change in life-style, or inconsistent visitation.

Typically, there are points of disruption beyond the two-year adjustment period, such as when mom or dad might start dating or maybe even get remarried. Yet this 28 percent of the children of divorce demonstrate a fairly healthy adjustment. In fact, two years after the divorce, this group cannot be distinguished from other children whose parents have remained together.

───── **M A K E I T Y O U R O W N** ─────

❶ What points of disruption have occurred in your family's life since the divorce? _____

_____

A second group of children of divorce (approximately 34 percent) go through the typical stages of grieving but spend more time in each of the stages. They don't reach a point of acceptance within a two-year time period but take anywhere from three to ten years.

This middle group usually includes children who have more family stresses to deal with than just their parents' divorce.

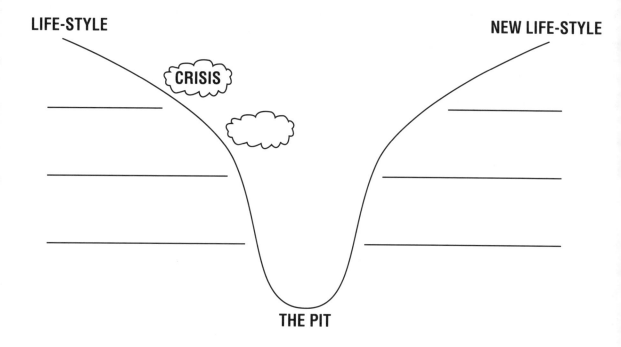

FIG. 2.6

CRISIS TIME LINE

LIFE-STYLE

NEW LIFE-STYLE

CRISIS

THE PIT

This middle category also can include children of divorce who experience "delayed reactions" to their parents' breakup. These children may seem fine for the first two years after their parents' separation, with little or no noticeable reaction. Yet three to five years later, with the onset of a new developmental stage (such as becoming a teenager), these kids will have a more severe reaction—testing limits, questioning authority, and distinguishing themselves as "troubled youth."

The long-term effects, which last into adulthood, are more noticeable for this group than for the first group discussed. They tend to show some effect from the divorce well into their adult lives, but effects that are noticeable only to close friends and confidants. These ongoing problems include difficulty with relationships, difficulty with trust, an imbalance accepting responsibility, and struggles with personal insecurities and achieving their full potential. These problems can affect their work, their friendships, marriages, and the way they raise their own children.

The good news is that, in time, these adult children of divorce eventually resolve their issues and live very normal adult lives. They marry, have children, and work in productive vocations.

————— **MAKE IT YOUR OWN** —————

❶ Which of the following complications has your family experienced since you became a single parent?

☐ A major move or major change in life-style (usually drastic decrease in financial status)

☐ Remarriage of one of the spouses and/or the blending of families

☐ A poor relationship with either parent

☐ A "messy divorce," such as a prolonged legal battle or custody fight

❷ What changes have you seen in your children related to these complications? _____

_____

_____

_____

The final group of children whose parents divorce (approximately 38 percent) consists of those who never seem to recover from the traumatic effects of their family's breakup. Their anger, depression, and general inability to accept their parents' divorce continue well into their adult lives. Their lack of adjustment can result in school failure, chronic unemployment, sometimes early marriages which end in divorce, other times an unwillingness to ever get married or have a family, an inability to trust others or to establish long-term relationships; and in the most extreme cases, a higher frequency of drug or alcohol abuse, personality disorders, and perhaps even criminal behaviors.

These statistics can be depressing, but we don't want to scare you. We want to challenge you.

The very fact that you're working through this book indicates that you want to help your kids through this process. That's a great start. Many of the parents in that third group are so wrapped up in their own problems that they can't be bothered with their children's emotional needs. You care.

You will not do everything right. No one does. After all, you are working through your own recovery process. How can you be perfectly honest, in control, strong with your kids, and respectful to your ex and still make a living? You will make some mistakes along the way. But honesty and forgiveness and love will cushion your fall.

And things may happen beyond your control. Your ex may be a real pain. You may encounter financial difficulties. Your kids may have trouble in school. In all honesty, such additional crises may set back your recovery, and that of your children. But recovery can still happen, even if on a somewhat different timetable.

These statistics tell us that two-thirds of those from divorced families make it to adulthood without major emotional scarring. That fact offers hope, as well as a challenge.

> Children have a good chance of overcoming the
> effects of divorce or the loss of a parent.

Are We a Dysfunctional Family?

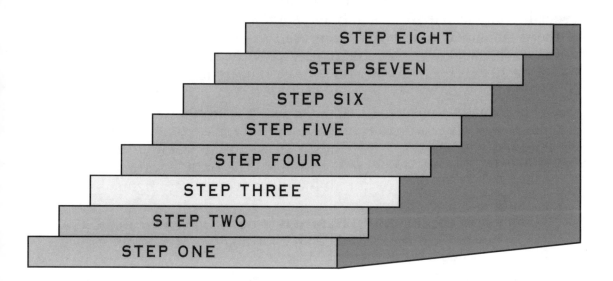

STEP THREE

*Honestly acknowledge your own "baggage,"
the unhealthy patterns you bring to
the family interaction, especially
with your children.*

Mike was 27 years old when I first met him at one of our church's social functions. He was friendly, but somewhat hesitant in anything other than superficial conversation. As I tried to get to know Mike over several weeks, he was able to peel away the layers and to expose more of his real self. As he did, a much different person began to emerge.

I eventually recognized that Mike had a drinking problem—not when he was with me, or anyone from the church for that matter. He had a totally different set of friends with whom he would drink and then usually get into some type of trouble. The trouble started with rowdiness and belligerence but all too often evolved into fights, broken windows, and eventual arrest.

I remember the first time I learned that he had spend the night in jail. I felt bad for him but asked, "What's going on? How could you pick a fight with a cop?"

Mike's response was one that I later heard over and over again, each time he got into trouble. "Well, when I was six years old my parents got a divorce. My dad took off with his secretary, and I didn't see him for three years." Mike would go on to explain how upsetting his childhood was, and how unfair it all seemed.

I remember saying, "Yeah, but Mike, that was 20 years ago. Isn't it time to move on with your life?"

Mike's response to my insensitive comment was filled with anger. "You don't understand! Nobody understands what it's like. Each time I get into a fight, or take a swing at a cop, I'm getting back at my dad...I'd like to kill him for what he did to me and my mom."

That comment pretty well summed up Mike's excuse each time he was thrown in jail or sent to a drug and alcohol rehabilitation center. Although I continued to reach out to Mike, he began to shut me out, following the pattern of all of his relationships.

I eventually lost touch with Mike for several years. Then I ran into him one morning in a coffee shop not too long ago. He had the same innocent, boyish grin, and once again seemed very standoffish at first. I asked him how he was doing and where he'd been for the past several years.

Mike proceeded to tell me that he had just gotten out of prison for a drunk driving conviction.

Surprised by this, I asked, "How did that happen?"

Mike, who was now over 30, recited a familiar response, "Well, when I was six years old my parents got a divorce...."

It would seem that Mike will never fully recover from his parents' divorce. His story, while probably more severe than most, is similar in its long-term effects to more than a third of the children of divorce.

Would Mike have had problems with drinking and self-control if his parents had never divorced? No one can really know for sure. Maybe the inclination was always there, and the divorce was only a catalyst for the problems. But the fact remains that Mike is continuing a pattern of irresponsibility. His father took no responsibility for the family he left behind, and now Mike takes no responsibility for himself. What will happen if Mike gets married? I'd like to think that the right woman might "turn him around." But I'm afraid that's a long shot. Mike is likely to continue the pattern, shirking the responsibility of marriage and walking out on his wife. And I think I know what he'll say: "Well, when I was six years old my parents got a divorce...."

In the current jargon of pop psychology, we could say that Mike came from a *dysfunctional* family. Simply put, "dysfunctional" means that it doesn't work. A dysfunctional clock doesn't tell the right time, a dysfunctional TV doesn't get all the channels, and a dysfunctional home doesn't have the proper atmosphere or support systems.

Reality would dictate that none of us grew up in a perfectly functional home or an absolutely dysfunctional home. We all fell somewhere on the continuum between functional and dysfunctional. If your home worked well most of the time, one would assume that

> A functional family is one in which unconditional love is expressed and family members are in harmony with one another.

you came from a functional family. That does not mean that there weren't dysfunctional aspects within your home—not always having open communication of emotions or the feeling that love was conditional at times. These imperfections are merely a natural part of the human condition.

However, some homes are *characterized* by dysfunction. In the dysfunctional home, relationships don't work. We typically see a lack of love, little expression of emotion, and little or no trust of family members. These symptoms often exist in homes where there has been physical or emotional abuse, substance abuse, or a difficult divorce.

——— MAKE IT YOUR OWN ———

❶ So where are you? Think about your family's situation, and then mark on the line below where you perceive your family to be.

dysfunctional   functional

1   2   3   4   5   6   7   8   9   10

❷ What characteristics make you think this? _____

_____

In my college days, my car's exhaust system started acting up. I didn't have money to get it fixed, so I asked a mechanically minded friend for help. He spotted a hole in the exhaust pipe and wrapped a tin can around it. That solved the problem! My car was functional again.

Two years later, a professional mechanic was fixing some other problem and asked me, "Did you know you have a tin can around your exhaust pipe?" He was mocking the fact that it wasn't a proper repair, but it had done the job.

That's the way it is in many single-parent and blended families. It's not perfect. Potential problems abound. But with proper attention to those problems, these families can piece together their home life so that it works. They *become* functional families even though their situations may be dysfunctional.

FAMILY OF ORIGIN

Divorce is hereditary. Research tells us that the divorce rate is much higher for those who came from difficult home environments. If your parents were divorced, or if you lost a parent at a young age, then that situation undoubtedly affected the way you dealt with relationships, with marriage, and with child-rearing. This is also the case for your children. If you are divorced, your children have a greater likelihood of going through a divorce themselves (about 60 percent), in spite of their determination that "it will never happen to me."

The Bible confirms this grim pattern. Deuteronomy 5:9 warns that "the iniquity of the fathers [is visited] upon the children to the third and fourth generations." But verse 10 implies that it doesn't have to be that way. The cycle can be broken. "But God [shows mercy]...to those who love Me and keep My commandments."

Family dysfunctions continue from one generation to the next. It is important for you to identify the dysfunctional characteristics in your home and try to correct them.

BARBARA (closet chocoholic)

MICHAEL (obsessively reads National Geographic)

TIMMY (pulls wings off flies)

ABBY (hoards food in crib mattress)

SCRUFFY (drinks from toilets)

THE SECRET LIFE OF THE NORMAL FAMILY

—— MAKE IT YOUR OWN ——

Let's get a general sense of how your family of origin worked.

❶ If you had to rate how your family worked as you were growing up, where on the line below would you rank your family's effectiveness?

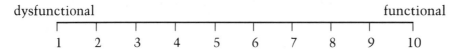

dysfunctional   functional

1   2   3   4   5   6   7   8   9   10

❷ If you could change one thing about how your family worked back then, what would it be? _____

_____

_____

❸ Look back to the continuum. How does your present family situation compare to the family in which you grew up? _____

❹ That one thing you would change if you could in your family of origin—is it present in your present family?

☐ A little

☐ Maybe, but in a disguised form

☐ Yes, it's an ongoing struggle

☐ Yes, it's a major problem

☐ Other. _____

_____

❺ As you raise your kids, in what ways are you *like* your parents as they raised you? Similarities:

1. _____
2. _____
3. _____
4. _____
5. _____

❻ How do you explain these similarities? Put the appropriate letter next to each similarity listed.

☐ a. Just my personal makeup

☐ b. Subconsciously the way I learned to be

☐ c. I've decided to be like this

☐ d. Other. _____

❼ In what ways do you *differ* from your parents, especially in child-rearing? Differences:

1. _____
2. _____
3. _____

4. _____

5. _____

❽ How would you explain these differences? Put the appropriate letter next to each difference listed.

☐ a. Just the way I am

☐ b. Subconsciously I learned that their way didn't work

☐ c. I decided not to be like them

☐ d. Other. _____

FACTORS THAT CONTRIBUTE TO DYSFUNCTION

1. Years of fighting in front of the children before an eventual divorce.

2. A particularly messy divorce, including court battles and ongoing custody fights.

3. One or both parents being particularly manipulative or controlling.

4. Any type of physical, sexual, or emotional abuse of you or your children.

5. Any type of substance abuse (alcohol, drugs, etc.) by one or both parents.

6. Prolonged family disruptions when the children are in their formative years (ages 1-10).

7. One parent who is in and out of the children's lives with no regularity or consistent love.

8. Vastly different parenting styles and conflicting values being taught to the children.

> Dysfunctions tend to carry over from one generation to the next. They can be changed.

As we learn more about specific dysfunctions, keep comparing your family of origin with your present family to see what you can learn. Never lose hope. You are not doomed to repeat your parents' mistakes. You can change things.

CHARACTERISTICS OF A DYSFUNCTIONAL FAMILY

Every home is different, and yet many dysfunctional families share common characteristics. Single parenting by itself does not create these dysfunctions. It's all the stuff that goes along with single parenting that makes your job so difficult. Here is just a partial list of factors that can intensify the difficulty. The more factors your family has experienced, the greater the likelihood is that it will be dysfunctional.

———— MAKE IT YOUR OWN ————

1 Look at the factors listed below. Consider how many factors were present in your family of origin, and how many have been present in your current family? For each factor present, rate it from 0 to 10 *in intensity* (10 being most intense).

	Family of Origin	Present Family
1. Predivorce fighting	_____	_____
2. Messy divorce	_____	_____
3. Manipulative/ controlling	_____	_____
4. Physical/Emotional Abuse	_____	_____
5. Substance abuse	_____	_____

	Family of Origin	Present Family
6. Family disruptions	_____	_____
7. In-and-out parent	_____	_____
8. Conflicting values	_____	_____
How many of these factors received a 5 or more?	_____	_____
What was the highest score listed?	_____	_____
ADD UP THE COLUMNS	_____	_____

Key:

Family of Origin

70 or more: Chances are, you have found significant problems in your relationships primarily due to traumas while growing up.

50–70: You've had to overcome some significant emotional baggage!

20–50: You may have some specific areas that were not what they should have been, but you must also have some areas of your family that were fairly functional.

0–20: You either are one of those rare ACONF's (Adult Children of Normal Families), or you just had one or two dysfunctional areas in an otherwise normal family.

Present Family

70 or more: You're working through some serious problems and will need to do a lot of work if your children are to overcome the effects.

50–70: You also have some serious issues to work through for yourself and your children.

20–50: You probably have one or two areas that need specific attention. Your children may seem to be fine, but unless you address these problem areas, they can have a potentially negative impact on your children.

0–20: While you have generally been spared the most serious consequences of divorce, you still need to look at some areas that need improvement. You have much to be thankful for.

LEARNING TO COPE

When these painful factors exist in a home, children learn to cope by building defense mechanisms to lessen the pain of their disappointments with their parents. These mechanisms may work well for them as youngsters, but in adult life they lead to problems and relational difficulties (thus the higher divorce rate). Let's look at a few examples to illustrate this point.

Case #1: Bob grew up in a single-parent home, the result of divorce. Now at the age of 25 he has difficulty expressing his emotions; in fact, he claims he is completely unaware of how he feels. In relationships, Bob has been accused of being insensitive and uncaring. He has been close to marriage twice but never tied the knot. Both relationships ended because the women involved said they became frustrated with Bob's inability to share anything about himself.

Bob grew up in a home with no father. He was raised by his mother and an aunt. They never really talked with him about his dad or anything about the earlier problems in the family. In order to "protect" Bob from the pain, the two women tried to shelter him from conflict, responsibilities, or emotional pain. Bob learned very early to not ask about anything that was not discussed with him, and therefore learned to block out his thoughts, feelings, and questions about personal matters. This worked quite well for Bob while growing up, but now he is in therapy in order to bring to the surface some feelings that have been buried for many years.

Case #2: Mindy's parents divorced when she was six. Her father left the home for another relationship, and Mindy's mom constantly reminded her of this for as long as she can remember. Mindy saw her dad from time to time but not with any kind of consistency. Her memory is that her dad tried to see her often in the beginning, but her mom fought him every step of the way until he finally gave up and only came around once in a while.

Not surprisingly, Mindy, now 28, has difficulty in relationships with men. She simply can't bring herself to trust them or make any type of commitment. She assumes that they will always let her down and eventually leave her, so she avoids the hurt by not letting herself care more than on a casual level.

Mindy learned to cope while growing up by not expecting anything from her dad and by not allowing herself to care. This served her well as a child, but as an adult it is interfering with her happiness in relationships.

Case #3: Monica grew up in a single-parent family. To complicate things, she was the oldest of six brothers and sisters. She had a lot of responsibilities in the home. She kept house, took care of a baby and three younger siblings, held down a part-time job, and contributed most of her earnings to the family budget. At age eighteen, when Monica finally broke free from her family, she went wild for a couple of years—in her words, "being totally irresponsible and caring only for myself."

Now at age 27, Monica works as a nurse and finds that she either mothers or controls everybody in her life. Her coworkers have felt her controlling influence, and her friends complain about her "mothering" tendencies. In dating relationships, Monica seems to choose men she can "rescue." They are chronically unemployed, in trouble, just out of jail, or alcoholic. She wonders why she picks the kind of men that she does.

From her home, Monica learned a sense of responsibility and how to take charge of a situation and keep it under control. In order to raise six brothers and sisters with no dad around and mom working ten hours a day, she had to. This behavior was appropriate for Monica while growing up, but how can she have healthier relationships now?

Case #4: Consider Matt. At age 35, Matt has been divorced twice and unemployed or underemployed most of his life. Matt does not believe he can do anything well and therefore goes into each new situation with an attitude of failure.

Matt's parents fought, sometimes violently, for as long as he can remember. They stayed together "for religious reasons" until he was fifteen years old. Then he was passed back and forth between his mom and dad (by court orders) for the next four years. He was in and out of college, then community college, then a technical school. He doesn't think he was really trained to do anything.

Growing up, Matt learned very early to run and hide whenever the harsh words started flying. He eventually learned that he was helpless to change his life or its circumstances, so consequently he became fatalistic. In other words, "I can't do anything to help myself, so I guess whatever happens, happens."

This attitude helped Matt to survive in a very dysfunctional home. But in adult life, Matt has two failed marriages and has never been successfully employed.

> Children learn to survive in a difficult home situation, but often the patterns they learn while growing up become detrimental to them in adult life. Their relationships tend to be dysfunctional.

——— MAKE IT YOUR OWN ———

❶ Which of the examples above most closely resembles your situation? (Check all that apply.)

☐ Bob (#1—can't express feelings)
☐ Mindy (#2—doesn't let herself care)
☐ Monica (#3—mothers everyone)
☐ Matt (#4—chronic underachiever)
☐ None of them really

❷ What coping mechanisms or defense systems did you learn in childhood that are inappropriate for life as an adult? _____

_____

_____

❸ In what areas do you see your children learning certain coping mechanisms or defense systems that may hurt them as adults? _____

DYSFUNCTIONAL CHARACTERISTICS

In examining some of the dysfunctional patterns from your own childhood and in your present family, we find some common characteristics often present in single-parent families. (For a more complete discussion of this topic, read *The Adult Child of Divorce* by Brissett and Burns. Copies are available from the Fresh Start office; 1-800-882-2799.)

▶ *Children from single-parent families do not know how a "normal" family functions*. Whether you are a single parent due to death, divorce, or being an unwed mother, your children in all likelihood will grow up without a strong sense of how an intact family operates. If your children hope to marry someday, how will they know how a husband or a wife acts within a loving, committed relationship? We can attribute your children's distorted view of reality to input from two extremes, both of which present an inaccurate portrayal of family life.

First, input from their own home is usually negative and distorted in terms of the role of the husband and father. If there is no father in the home, or even a strained relationship between mom and dad, then probably they will have distorted views of how husbands and wives interact.

The second place that children from single-parent families gain their distorted perceptions of family is from the television. If they grew up with "The Brady Bunch" or "Family Ties," then they learned that families have problems sometimes, but that families resolve those problems within the half-hour. When these children eventually marry, they are ill-prepared for the complexities of relationships and normal family interactions. Thus, the divorce rate is higher for children of divorce.

———— **MAKE IT YOUR OWN** ————

❶ How much time do your children spend in the home of an intact family? _____

❷ What might you do to further such exposure? _____

_____

❸ Who provides male role models in your children's lives? _____

_____

❹ What experiences in problem-solving are your children receiving within the family? _____

_____

_____

Single-parent children have difficulty with trust. Research by Judith Wallerstein has tracked children of divorce for twenty years following the breakup of their families. She found that children of divorce, especially the girls, have difficulty in trusting others, particularly the opposite sex. This lack of trust has led to a lack of committed relationships, a lack of trust for parents and other authority figures, and eventually to delayed marriages.

Wallerstein's research correlates this trait with a poor relationship with dad, particularly when the child has experienced some sense of betrayal—a mom or dad who has lied or been inconsistent with the children, and with parents who tell their children "sugarcoated" versions of the truth. An example of this last trait would be a mom who tells her kids that everything is fine, and that they don't have to worry about a thing, when in reality the finances are poor, the home is a wreck, and Mom is falling apart. Another example is the dad who takes the kids to a carnival every time he sees them and does not provide the structure of a normal parenting relationship. Even though dad believes this will endear him to his children, it merely creates a superficial relationship separated from the reality of everyday life.

—— MAKE IT YOUR OWN ——

❶ In what ways do you find yourself sugarcoating the truth? _____

_____

_____

❷ In what ways does the noncustodial parent seem to provide carnival time for the children? _____

_____

_____

▶ *Children from single-parent families have a tendency toward low self-worth and chronic underachievement.* The Wallerstein research has uncovered a tendency in children of divorce, particularly the boys, to have a low sense of self-worth, which may perpetuate a negative cycle of failure. These children do not reach their academic potential, have difficulty in making college and career decisions, flounder in college or vocational schools, and then are chronically underemployed.

Research links these traits to a lack of affirmation while growing up, an insecure home environment where a dad or mom is viewed as being unreliable, and homes where there has been excessive fighting or "bad-mouthing," which spills over onto the kids.

▶ *Single-parent children can be overly responsible.* The Wallerstein study finds this trait most prevalent in girls. These children grow up feeling responsible for everyone around them. They feel that their parents' divorce was somehow their fault, their mother's loneliness is their responsibility, and maybe even the household finances their concern. They overburden themselves with thoughts of how they are going to keep the family together, to the point that they begin to parent their parents. This role reversal is compounded when parents begin to confide in their children, to use their children as buddies or counselors. Children are just not ready for the adult world and adult problems.

The overburdened child is most often the eldest daughter, the son who is "the man of the house," and the latchkey kid who has always had to fend for himself or herself.

———— **MAKE IT YOUR OWN** ————

❶ What expectations do you have of your child(ren)? _____

_____

_____

_____

❷ Do most of these expectations center around

☐ school work

☐ home chores

☐ social life

☐ family support

☐ other _____

_____

❸ When are your expectations least often met? _____

_____

_____

▶ *The single-parent child can be irresponsible or rebellious.* This characteristic is a result of the same or similar dynamics to the preceding trait, but is more common in boys. In these cases the children become angry about the increased responsibilities, and they rebel against the system. In some cases, the child may take on the responsibilities for a while, and then reverse direction in an explosion of anger that has been building up.

One girl I know is, I believe, a ticking time bomb of responsibility just waiting to explode into freedom. She has taken on all of her mother's responsibilities and is extremely compliant. All those around her consider her to be very mature for her age, but I sense a great deal of seething anger just under the surface. She will be leaving for college soon, and I just hope that she can ease into a more normal life-style rather than explode into rebelliousness that might get her into some serious trouble.

▶ *Children from single-parent families have difficulty with open communication.* Not all single-parent families cultivate this difficulty. However, typically, in homes where there has been dysfunction and strife, children learn a set of rules that much recovery literature has documented. The three rules:

▶ Don't talk

▶ Don't feel

▶ Don't trust

Children learn "don't talk." They find out that it is not okay to question or to bring up certain issues in front of one or both parents. It is often difficult to talk about the other parent (especially if that parent is doing well) and about the problems that led to the breakup. This "gag rule" on certain issues may be news to you as the parent, but I can assure you that your children are very aware of the taboo subjects.

"Don't feel" is an extension of a lack of communication about certain issues and refers to the child's inability to talk about their feelings: their love for Dad, how they feel about Mom's new boyfriend and how they feel about being put in the middle of loyalty conflicts. Children learn that it is too costly to express how they really feel, so they withdraw emotionally and begin what can be a life-long cycle of repression.

"Don't trust" takes the lack of communication to its logical conclusion. If one cannot talk about certain issues and does not feel free to express his or her emotions, then it is only a matter of time before trust deteriorates.

─────── MAKE IT YOUR OWN ───────

❶ What areas of your lives together would you prefer that your children not talk about? _____

_____

_____

_____

Look at your list, and circle those areas that you also have difficulty talking about.

❷ What areas are the same for both? _____

_____

❸ What loyalty conflicts have arisen in your family? _____

_____

4 How were these conflicts resolved? _____

▶ *The single-parent family tends toward role reversals, a lack of clear boundaries, and constant transitions.* Children in single-parent families will tend to take on so many new responsibilities within the home that they are actually parenting their parents. The equilibrium of a two-parent home has been shaken, and now the custodial parent needs someone else to fill the gaps. A son may become the "man of the house." A daughter may become mom's confidante and counselor. What makes these role reversals even more difficult is the fact that the roles are constantly changing.

The lack of boundaries is seen not only in the children's taking parental roles, but blurry parent/child interactions. Instead of seeing their parents as stable and in control, children in single-parent families see their parents in vulnerable, sometimes compromising positions.

These ongoing role changes in the family keep the children from feeling the safety and security that they might otherwise feel in a more stable, well-defined home.

CHARACTERISTICS OF FAMILIES

Functional	vs	Dysfunctional
1. Models of "normal" family relationships		Distorted family perceptions
2. Trusting, committed relationships		Lack of trust
3. Mature view of self and reaching full potential		Low self-image, chronic underachievement
4-5. Acceptance of age-appropriate responsibilities		Either super-responsible (4) or irresponsible (5)
6. Open, honest communication		Lack of honest expression of feelings
7. Clear roles and boundaries within the family		Roles reversed or constantly changing

---

We've talked about the continuum of functional and dysfunctional. *All* families are dysfunctional in some way, to some degree. But single-parent families are especially susceptible to dysfunctions.

Below are seven lines stretched between functional models and dysfunctional models. As you look at your children, where along those lines would they be? Take time to observe them, maybe even talk with them about this. Then mark with an X the appropriate spots on those lines.

Functional		*Dysfunctional*
1. Models of "normal" family relationships	————————	Distorted family perceptions
2. Trusting, committed relationships	————————	Lack of trust
3. Mature view of self, reaching potential	————————	Low self-image, underachievement
4-5. Acceptance of age-appropriate responsibilities	———————— ————————	Super-responsible Irresponsible
6. Open communication	————————	Lack of honest expression of feelings
7. Clear roles and boundaries in family	————————	Roles reversed or constantly changing

❶ Which area is of greatest concern? ————————————
————————————————————————————

❷ What symptoms of the negative behavior do you see? ————
————————————————————————————
————————————————————————————

❸ What do you think you can do about this? _____

_____

_____

❹ Write the answer to this final question in the form of a goal and include it in your list of "Action Points" in appendix A. _____

_____

_____

_____

Breaking the Cycle

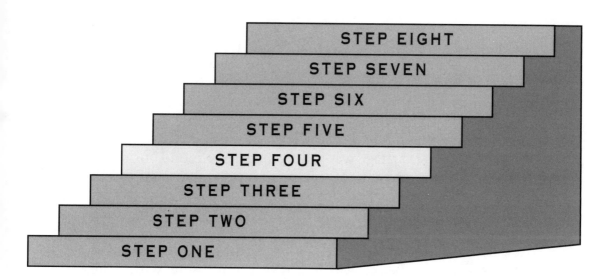

STEP FOUR

Determine to develop new, healthier patterns of parenting.

Becky was one of the most normal people I'd ever known. At least that's what I thought before she came in for counseling. She had a great sense of humor, she seemed quite stable, but most of all she impressed me as a great mom.

In counseling she revealed that she had come from a very dysfunctional home: a lot of emotional abuse and some physical abuse. Now her own marriage was falling apart. She found out that her husband was bisexual and actively pursuing other relationships. When she could tolerate it no longer, she asked him to move out. While he moved out willingly, he vowed he'd make her pay for forcing him out of his home.

Becky's husband got his revenge by refusing to pay any type of support, even though Becky was a stay-at-home mom with a large mortgage. It wasn't long before she was months behind on her bills. Subsequently, her home and all of her possessions were sold in a sheriff's sale. The courts could do nothing to help her and her two girls other than to offer them beds in a homeless shelter. Her only option was to move back into her parents' home.

When she told me this, explaining that it really was a "bad scene" at home, I thought, "Yeah, I'd hate to move back home too, but you do what you have to do." Becky asked me to inquire at church for a family who might be willing to take in a mother and her two daughters. I told her I would but knew that finding such a situation would be difficult.

I left word with the pastoral staff and the deacon board. In the meantime, Becky took a job at just above minimum wage, though she hated leaving her children at home with her parents. She also learned that her former husband was in jail for a sex offense.

Becky called me regularly every week to ask about news on housing. Each week I had the same discouraging response, to which she would reply, "Please find me something soon. Living with my folks is really not working out."

After several weeks Becky stopped calling. I assumed things had stabilized at home, and that Becky was now fine. But then I ran into one of her friends. "Did you hear about Becky? She came home from work one day, and her kids had been beaten so badly by her father that they needed medical attention. She then took her kids and moved in with a man she had just met. Becky said, 'At least he cares for me and my children.'"

I was speechless. My thoughts gravitated to the questions that have haunted me since I heard the news. What could I have done, and why in a church of 1,800 people, could we not find help for one single parent who was in need?

I don't condone Becky's decision, but I came to realize that she merely responded to the most basic of human drives—the need to protect one's children and oneself. She had appealed to her church, and we were unable or unwilling to help her. So she made a decision that I believe under normal circumstances she would never have made.

That Sunday as I sat in the worship service, we sang, "They Will Know We Are Christians by Our Love." A lump grew in my throat as I sang the words, and tears came to my eyes. How could we point fingers at a woman like Becky until we had examined our own lives?

Becky recognized that she came from a dysfunctional home, and she tried to break that cycle with her children. It's not that easy.

HOW TO BREAK THE DYSFUNCTIONAL CYCLE

People from dysfunctional homes tend to marry dysfunctional people and get involved in dysfunctional systems—such as cult-like churches, codependent friendships, and manipulative relationships. That is probably why Becky initially married a man with serious problems and may be repeating that cycle in her new relationship.

Since she isn't sure what a healthy relationship looks like, she gravitates toward relationships that are familiar—dysfunctional ones.

The first step in breaking the cycle for you and your children is for you to recognize the dysfunction of your family of origin, to examine how you display the same characteristics, and to determine to change them.

Step One: Recognize Your Own Dysfunction and Determine to Change

In the last chapter you identified unhealthy patterns from the past and how they have affected you.

You need to explore these dysfunctional patterns even further to be sure you don't have a "blind spot" about some family characteristic that you think is normal.

———— MAKE IT YOUR OWN ————

❶ Have you asked a friend or counselor for an outside perspective on any "blind spot" dysfunctions in your family?

☐ Need to do. Whom will I ask? _____

☐ Have done. Who helped me? _____

What did I learn? _____

_____

_____

❷ What are some of the areas I need to work on? _____

_____

_____

After your personal and family evaluation, which may take some time, the next element is your determination to make a difference with your children. Even though you probably cannot change your basic personality, you can determine to act differently toward others.

Step Two: Focus On Your Own Recovery

One of the best ways to help your children is to recover from your own difficult past. Whether it is divorce, abuse, or a critical spirit, you must overcome its effects on you if you are to avoid passing on these traits. A review of the major recovery programs finds three common healing themes for those who are recovering.

▶a twelve-step recovery program

▶a spiritual renewal

▶some kind of accountability or support group

Let me summarize these:

Twelve-Step Recovery:

a. We admit that we have a problem and are powerless to change by ourselves. (Step 1)

b. We come to realize that only God can change us, so we turn our lives over to Him. (Steps 2 and 3)

c. We examine our lives, admit our wrongdoings to God and others, and try to live in obedience to God. (Steps 4, 5, 6)

d. We seek forgiveness and make amends to those we have wronged and ask God to renew our minds to be more like Him. (Steps 7, 8, 9, 10)

e. We seek to grow in our relationship with God and try to help others by telling them of God's healing power and grace. (Steps 11 and 12)

Here are the original twelve steps:

The Twelve Steps of Alcoholics Anonymous*

1. We admitted we were powerless over alcohol—that our lives had become unmanageable.

*The Twelve Steps are reprinted with permission of Alcoholics Anonymous World Services, Inc. Permission to reprint the Twelve Steps does not mean that AA has reviewed or approved the content of this publication, nor that AA agrees with the views expressed herein. AA is a program of recovery from alcoholism—use of the Twelve Steps in connection with programs and activities which are patterned after AA, but which address other problems, does not imply otherwise.

2. Came to believe that a Power greater than ourselves could restore us to sanity.

3. Made a decision to turn our will and our lives over to the care of God as we understood Him.

4. Made a searching and fearless moral inventory of ourselves.

5. Admitted to God, to ourselves, and to another human being the exact nature of our wrongs.

6. Were entirely ready to have God remove all these defects of character.

7. Humbly asked Him to remove our shortcomings.

8. Made a list of all persons we had harmed, and became willing to make amends to them all.

9. Made direct amends to such people wherever possible, except when to do so would injure them or others.

10. Continued to take personal inventory and when we were wrong promptly admitted it.

11. Sought through prayer and meditation to improve our conscious contact with God as we understood Him, praying only for knowledge of His will for us and the power to carry that out.

12. Having had a spiritual awakening as the result of these steps, we tried to carry this message to alcoholics, and to practice these principles in all our affairs.

—————— **MAKE IT YOUR OWN** ——————

Examine the 12 steps to recovery.

❶ Which steps have you taken in your life? Put a + beside each of them.

❷ Which steps do you still need to take? Put a − beside those.

❸ What one action will you take in the coming week to speed you on the road to recovery? _____

Spiritual Renewal: Just as the Twelve Steps imply, true recovery can only take place in conjunction with a spiritual renewal. Without a personal relationship with God, you are powerless to change yourself or even to forgive those who have wronged you. But what does it mean to have this kind of relationship with God? The Bible tells us that God freely accepts us on the basis of His grace, as displayed by His sending His Son to die in our place.

How do we accept such a gift? The Bible clearly states that we obtain this gift from God by trusting in Christ as our personal Savior—accepting His death as payment in full for all our sins. Rejecting our own good works and accepting God's grace is what many people refer to as being "born again." This new birth assures us that we will be spending eternity with God in heaven, and also empowers us to begin living a new life-style; one that is committed to becoming more and more like Christ.

——— MAKE IT YOUR OWN ———

We often find ourselves struggling under the weight of burdens we can no longer support.

❶ What burdens, or areas of your life, are you ready to release to God's care? _____

_____

_____

_____

❷ What disciplines are you ready to assume to further your spiritual renewal?
☐ Prayer (Private)
☐ Prayer (Corporate/as in worship)
☐ Bible reading

❸ How have you felt God's power at work in your life? _____

_____

❹ Can you give one concrete example of how God has helped you and brought about some change in your life or in the lives of your children? _____

_____

_____

_____

Accountability and Support: Another important element in any recovery program is the idea of ongoing support and accountability. Those in recovery from some type of addiction usually attend weekly AA meetings or a similar group. In addition, they usually have a sponsor who checks on them and befriends them through the more difficult periods. This same idea is essential for our own recovery.

In Christian circles we call this concept "discipleship." We try to help and encourage one another to grow in Christ through one-on-one relationships and through regular fellowship with other believers. Find a trusted friend, or a group of friends, with whom you can share your heart.

———— MAKE IT YOUR OWN ————

❶ Whom can you identify as a trusted friend who will offer support:

at work? _____

at church? _____

in the neighborhood? _____

other? _____

Step Three: Work On Healthy Parenting Skills

The patterns we developed while growing up or exercised while we were married may not be the best ones now that we are trying to parent alone. For some, the absence of a spouse will be a significant loss in terms of helping with the parenting process. For others, the absence of a spouse may make it easier for you to parent in a positive way. Gone are the mixed messages, the unpredictable behaviors, and the sporadic discipline.

Before you blame your former spouse for all of the dysfunctional behaviors in the house, remember that in general, dysfunctional people choose dysfunctional spouses. Together, they perpetuate dysfunctional family systems. One of your tasks as a single parent is to focus on the areas in which you can improve.

> You can break the cycle of dysfunction with your children. It takes the courage to see the dysfunctions in your own home, determination to change things, diligence to seek your own recovery, honesty to be accountable to others, and dedication to new parenting skills.

———— MAKE IT YOUR OWN ————

We can all work harder on our parenting skills. Even if you do not feel responsible for creating problems with your children, still you can work on some issues.

In which of the following areas can you improve?
- ☐ Open communication with my children
- ☐ Active listening skills
- ☐ Demonstration of unconditional love
- ☐ Consistent discipline
- ☐ Keeping your word
- ☐ Building your child's self-image
- ☐ Modeling Christ-like behaviors

MAKING A DIFFERENCE WITH YOUR CHILDREN

Parenting as a single does not differ a lot from parenting in general. Both require loving discipline, guidance, modeling, nurturing, teaching, and a full range of emotional support. The greatest difference is twofold:

1. your children tend to be more emotionally needy because of their sense of loss, and

2. you don't have the additional support of a second parent who can share your decisions and frustrations.

You need to focus on a few critical skills that will produce characteristics of a functional family.

Rebuild "Normal" Trusting Relationships

One of the greatest divorce casualties is the ability to trust again, at least in the immediate aftermath. This is true for children as well as adults. As a parent, it is primarily *your* responsibility to rebuild your children's trust, since you are probably the most influential adult in their lives. You may also be the target of their distrust, especially if you were the one who left, or if you are perceived as having betrayed the family in some way.

Rebuilding trust takes time and requires complete honesty from you. Demonstrate honesty in the way you explain divorce to your children, how you share your feelings, and by keeping your word.

To compensate the children for the losses experienced in the divorce, some parents compound the mistake by making promises that they are not sure they can keep. Promises of vacations, trips to Disney World, and extravagant toys may be desperate attempts to show the children that you love them. If not followed through, they reinforce the belief that mom or dad can't be trusted.

You must realize that now your life is under a microscope. Your children are testing to see if they can trust you again. Measure your words before you speak. These promises include the negative ones, too. You might tell your children, "If I hear you whine one more time, I'll send you to your room for a month." Don't say it unless you can follow through on your word! This might seem like a minor infraction, one we have all been guilty of. But now, more than ever, it is imperative that you think before you speak.

—— MAKE IT YOUR OWN ——

Think about the following statements:

"If you do that one more time, I'll kill you!"

"If you don't clean your plate, you won't eat for a week."

"If you don't get in the car right now, I'll never take you shopping again."

Think about the message these words convey to your children regarding their ability to trust you.

❶ What could you say to your children after making such threats to them in a moment of frustration? _____

_____

_____

_____

❷ What are some statements that build trust because they demonstrate our respect for our children and what they are feeling? _____

_____

_____

_____

Another way to rebuild trusting relationships is to surround your children with good, healthy role models. These can include a youth pastor, a church leader, a teacher, a Scout leader, or a coach. Carefully consider the type of people you want your children to spend time with, and then put them in proximity to those people by having them join the YMCA or a Scouting program, attend Christian school, or a church youth retreat. While all of these choices cost you money, you will want to count the cost and determine your priorities.

MAKE IT YOUR OWN

Think about the various aspects of your children's lives. Within each area, list the positive and negative role models.

FIG. 4.1

	ROLE MODELS	
Area of Life	**Positive**	**Negative**
Family		
Friends		
School		
Church		
Extracurricular activities: sports scouting hobbies clubs		

❶ What activities might you encourage?

___

___

___

Provide a Loving Environment for Your Children

A loving environment is one of the most important gifts you can give to your children. However, many would disagree as to what a loving environment entails. Should we be firm or compassionate; foster independence or reliance on the family; give in to their wishes or force them to "do without"? The important point is that you assure your children of your unconditional love for them.

Unconditional love for a child of divorce must come in the form of constant reassurance of your love and commitment to their well-being. They need to know that you will be there for them, and that they are a top priority, even though you have other responsibilities that require your time. They need to see concrete expressions of that love during the good times and the bad.

Practical expressions of that love might include

▶Verbal reassurance of *specific* things that you like about each child. Not just, "You're a great kid," but "I like your sense of humor."

▶Physical contact with your child, including hugs, kisses, back scratching, etc. This contact is important from both mom and dad, so that your children grow up with a strong sense of affection and appropriate touch.

▶Notes and cards that express pleasure with something they have done, or something you like about their personality. (This is particularly helpful for the noncustodial parent to do.)

▶Individual time spent with each child. Find a hobby or activity that you can share with each child alone. For example, you might take turns taking each of your children out for breakfast.

▶Listening actively to your children. Focus on them and what they are saying. Stop what you are doing and give them good eye contact. Do not give advice or simplistic answers, but try to view the information through their eyes.

▶Frequent phone calls (for the noncustodial parent) during the week that focus on them and their day. Also, give them a number where you can be reached at almost any time. They need to be assured that they have easy access to you when they feel they need to talk about something.

No one displays unconditional love at all times. However, if this is your goal, then you also need to ask for forgiveness when you "lose it" with your kids. If you grew up in a home that was less than loving, then you might have particular difficulty expressing this love to your children. [For a more in-depth look at learning how to love your children, I would recommend *How to Really Love Your Child*, by Ross Campbell.]

—————— **M A K E I T Y O U R O W N** ——————

❶ In which of the following ways have you expressed love to your child(ren) *in the last week*?

☐ Verbal reassurance of *specific* things that you like about each child.

What were they? _____

_____

☐ Physical contact with your child, including hugs, kisses, back scratching.

☐ Notes and cards that expressed pleasure with something they had done, or something you like about their personality.

☐ Individual time spent with each child.

☐ Listening actively to your children.

When?_____

What were they saying? _____

_____

Provide Firm, yet Loving Discipline

It is very hard to maintain discipline in a single-parent family (assuming you ever had it). As they lose touch with their children or lose the energy to keep up with their rowdiness, many parents take the easy way out—they give in or react in haste. Yet the child of divorce needs discipline to feel secure and loved. Discipline also helps maintain proper boundaries.

Appropriate boundaries are essential, if your new family is to work properly. Many single parents scrap discipline to be their children's friends. Absentee dads can make the mistake of using their precious time for fun only, forgetting about homework, bedtime, and other parental responsibilities. Custodial moms on the other hand might mistakenly make a son "the man of the house," entrusting him with adult responsibilities, or confiding in a daughter as a best friend. A close relationship is fine, but it becomes dysfunctional when your children can no longer be children but must take on adult roles before they are emotionally ready to cope.

Hold a family meeting soon after the other parent leaves the home, in order to discuss the future organization of the family and the expectations of each member. Everyone will need to take on new responsibilities. Discuss consequences for misbehavior, as well as a schedule for leisure time, bedtime, homework, and daily chores. The initial meeting is most effective if *both* parents can participate. It is best for your children if they have consistent discipline and expectations in both family settings. While this kind of cooperation is rare among single parents, it is critical for breaking the cycle of dysfunction.

I will review a few guidelines for balanced discipline:

▶ "Make the punishment fit the crime." Don't overreact to minor infractions, and take seriously the mistakes which carry long-term implications.

Logical consequences make the most sense and also teach valuable lessons, such as:

"If you don't put away your toys, I'll have to put them up for a couple of days."

"If you don't turn off the Nintendo now, you won't be allowed to play with it tomorrow."

"Since I don't like to see you act that way, why don't you sit in the other room until you're through pouting?"

The consequences for each situation require thought and patience. Stay calm and do not react in the anger of the moment. The easiest thing to do is not always the best.

▶ "Pick your battlegrounds." This simple phrase expresses the need for you to decide which areas are important enough to "battle" over. This is particularly true of teenagers. Since discipline takes a lot of thought and energy, you may decide not to battle over "cleaning your plate," or whether your daughter can wear makeup to school. Decide in advance which issues are important and on which you need to show some latitude.

▶Distinguish between accidents, disobedience, and defiance. Even though accidents may be devastating to you personally, don't deal with them as harshly as disobedience or defiance.

For example, if my daughter spills her juice on my computer and ruins it, I'm going to be very upset. (Especially if I'm at the end of a long document that I haven't saved to the disk yet.) Her seeing how upset I am may be punishment enough. In fact, I'll probably end up hugging her and assuring her that "It's okay; I realize that it was an accident."

However, if I tell her to sit in the kitchen and drink her juice, and instead she walks into my office and spills her juice, I need to punish her for disobedience. Perhaps sitting her in her chair for a while is an appropriate punishment, even though my anger at the moment might make me want to do more.

The most serious infraction is defiance and therefore deserves the harshest consequences.

If my daughter looks me right in the eye and pours the juice on my computer right after I tell her to take her juice back to the kitchen, that is defiance. For that, a young child might be spanked or restricted to her room. An older child might even have to work to replace the computer he or she has ruined (a logical consequence of the defiant action).

As you can see from the example, the result is the same. My computer is ruined. What I must discern is whether it was an accident, disobedience, or defiance.

▶Punish the deed, not the doer. Explain to your children the difference between your feelings toward them and your feelings about their behavior. Tell your children, "I love you, but I don't like the way you are behaving."

Remember when your parents used to say, "This is going to hurt me more than it will hurt you," just before they spanked you? Even though it drove you crazy at the time. I believe the message behind the words is valid. The message is "Because I love you, I have to do this. But it hurts me, too."

When you react to your child's misbehavior, be careful to express your love for the child while also making your displeasure with the deed clear. Often you'll want to modify your immediate reaction.

"You're acting like a stupid idiot" might become "I know you are very capable, but the way you're acting right now isn't very smart."

"Shut up!" could be stated, "I want to listen to you, but could you please stop talking right now so that I can think?

"I hate it when you do that!" might need to be changed to "I love you, but I don't like it when you do that."

Such modifications seem obvious in the calm reality of the present, but they take great willpower and thought when you reach the height of your frustration.

─────── **MAKE IT YOUR OWN** ───────

❶ What was the most recent incident of disciplining your children when you did the following (or, if you can't come up with these examples, consider when and how you *should* have):

a. made the punishment fit the crime _____

_____

_____

b. picked a worthwhile battleground _____

_____

_____

c. distinguished accidents from disobedience or defiance _____

_____

_____

d. explained the difference between your feelings about your child's behavior and your love for your child _____

_____

_____

❷ What might be appropriate punishments for the following misbehaviors:

Staying out past curfew? _____

Speaking disrespectfully to you? _____

"Forgetting" to do homework? _____

Ignoring household chores? _____

Fighting with a brother or sister? _____

_____

❸ How might you rephrase the following comments to reassure a child of your love, in the midst of disapproval?

"You are such a klutz! Why can't you hold on to those dishes?"

_____

"I hate you when you sass me like that!" _____

_____

"NO! Didn't you hear what I said? You can't go to the movies tonight!" _____

_____

_____

Some helpful books that take a closer look at issues of disciplining your children are *Dare to Discipline* and *The Strong-Willed Child* by James Dobson, and *The Power of a Parent's Words* by H. Norman Wright.

Foster Healthy Relationships

It is very important that you promote healthy role models for your children—role models that will help you break the cycle of divorce and dysfunction. This practice includes monitoring their friends, finding positive opposite sex and same sex adult relationships, and providing some exposure to healthy, intact families.

Insist on meeting your children's friends. Even if they are teenagers, you are entitled to know who your children are spending time with. Try to be friendly and open-minded toward all of them.

Try to put your children in places where they will be with a more desirable peer group; such as a church group, the YMCA, specific clubs, or even civic groups. However, their involvement with these positive peer groups does not negate your need to know your children, their friends, and what they're up to.

When it comes to adult role models, find those who will be a stable and reliable influence. This role is especially important if your former mate does not provide that type of support. A role model of the opposite sex is critical. Choose a family friend, a grandparent, an uncle; someone you can count on to be there for them over the long haul. Do not fill this role with a series of boyfriends or girlfriends who might happen to be in your life. These relationships only perpetuate the notion that men (or women) can't be trusted.

If a friend of the opposite sex does take an interest in your children, then it is best that the person be primarily interested in helping your children and not trying to get closer to you. If no one has shown a real interest in fulfilling this role, you might want to ask a friend or relative specifically to help out. They might not realize the need and would be flattered that you asked.

Although many of your friendships will move away from married couples and toward singles, maintain relationships with some healthy married couples. It is good for both you and your children to observe happily married couples, so that you don't lose your perspective.

One teenager recently told me, "I don't know if I'll ever get married. I don't know of a single family where there hasn't been a divorce, or of one of that isn't headed in that direction."

Another girl told me, "I'm real nervous around men. I've never lived in a home with a man because my dad left when I was three. Whenever I'm around couples, I always check out the husband and wife to see how they act. I want to know what a normal family looks like for when I get married. That is, if that ever happens."

Special times with relatives and friends who are married, both during holidays and when they're just doing their daily routine, can be an important part of your child's development.

———— MAKE IT YOUR OWN ————

❶ What's the healthiest relationship your child has right now? _____

_____

_____

❷ In general, how do you feel about your children's friends? _____

_____

_____

❸ Is there anything you can do (if you need to) to improve your child's friendships? _____

_____

_____

_____

4 Does your child have a positive role model of the opposite sex? If so, who? _____

If not, is there someone you know who can fill this role? _____

5 What models of marriage does your child have? Is there a happily married couple you are friendly with? _____

_____

_____

6 In what ways can you maximize your child's exposure to such healthy relationship models? _____

_____

_____

Build a Positive Sense of Self-worth

No matter what your job, your most important responsibility is rearing your children. One of the greatest gifts you can pass on to your children is a balanced self-image.

Of all of the problems that I face in counseling and in day-to-day contact with people, the most prevalent and pervasive is that of insecurity or poor self-image. To some extent, we *all* struggle with this from time to time.

Each of us must ask, "What does our society value in a person, and what values do I reinforce in my home?" Unfortunately, in most settings, children see that they are valued primarily in four areas: beauty, brains, brawn, and bucks. Our society reflects those values in everything from advertising and cartoons to who gets elected to the local school board.

If children are not good-looking or smart, they often feel like failures, and classmates may treat them that way. This is particularly true for girls. Boys, on the other hand, can get away with not being exceptionally handsome or smart as long as they are good at sports.

The fourth area of value—bucks—is one that we adults know well. Yet you may be surprised at how important money is to a child's popularity and standing with his or her peers. Our children must wear the right clothes, have the latest games and toys, and even have the correct label on their sneakers. Children are also keenly aware of who lives in the "right" neighborhoods and whose parents are influential in the community.

If a child does not have at least one of the four ingredients—beauty, brains, brawn, or bucks—then he or she is destined to an uphill struggle in order to achieve acceptance in our society. How can you help your children develop positive self-images?

▶Love yourself so that you can properly love your children. If *you* do not have a good self-image, then your first task is to get help for yourself, so that you can model a positive self-image to your children.

▶Counterbalance what their peer group values. Show them a more secure kind of love: one that values and loves them all the time.

▶Nurture your children with physical attention and concrete expressions of love. Mention specific things you like about each child.

▶Encourage your children to be open and honest with their feelings. Don't negate their feelings even when you disagree with them. You need to be an example of open and honest communication.

▶Foster independence in your child. Encourage their decision-making and willingness to try things on their own, even when you think it might lead to failure. When they do fail, allow them to suffer the consequences. Be there for them emotionally, encouraging them to try again.

Give Your Children a Sense of Purpose or Meaning in Their Lives

Children and adults *need* something in their lives that gives them meaning and purpose. For some, it is their work. For others it may be service to other people. Still others seek a personal relationship with God. Whatever your pursuit, you have probably come to find that living solely for "me and my needs" is an unfulfilling, selfish quest. Many have found greater fulfillment when they live their lives for something beyond themselves—to glorify God with their lives.

One of the failures of the yuppie generation was their pursuit of wealth and power, devoid of ethical considerations. King Solomon, one of the richest and most powerful men of his time, said, "All that the world has to offer is a vain pursuit." As we teach our children how to make their way in this world, we must not forget that a faith or belief system should be part of the fabric of our lives. We have an obligation to present a firm set of values to our children, which tell them who we are and why we are here.

Young children will not understand these concepts, and your teenagers will rebel against them. So many parents ask, "Why bother?".

Children may not understand the depth of your faith in God now or may not want to hear about it later, but the seeds you plant today will have a big influence on how they live as adults. And the best way to teach a belief system, or your faith in God, is to live it.

———— MAKE IT YOUR OWN ————

1 Rate your kids in the following areas. What advantages do they have in:

	Dismal	Below avg	Avg	Above avg	Exceptional
beauty					
brains					
brawn					
bucks					

Which of these do you think your child's peers value the most? _____ the least? _____

How do you think this affects your child's self-image? _____

_____

_____

2 To what extent does your child have a sense of meaning in life?
- ☐ Very much so. My child is very secure and directed.
- ☐ About average, I guess.
- ☐ Good days, bad days.

☐ Not at all. My child seems aimless, insecure.

Other? _____

❸ Do you think your child's friends have *more* or *less* of a sense of meaning in life than your child does? _____

Do you have a sense of meaning in your life?

☐ Very much so. I am very secure and directed.

☐ About average, I guess.

☐ Good days, bad days.

☐ Not at all. My life seems aimless, insecure.

Other? _____

❹ We've talked in this workbook about a "relationship with God." If you had to describe your relationship with God in three words, what words would you choose? _____

_____

❺ On a scale of 0 to 100, how much desire do you have to improve your relationship with God (100 being most)? _____

Why? _____

❻ If you desire to, what can you do to improve your relationship with God? _____

_____

What effect do you think that would have on your child? _____

_____

_____

❼ In what ways could you do a better job of teaching your beliefs to your children? _____

_____

_____

❽ How much would it help to surround yourself and your children with people who share your beliefs? _____

_____

_____

How could you do this? _____

_____

_____

Action Point: If you'd like to develop your relationship with God, and you're not sure how, here's a plan.

1. Talk to Him. Each day for the next week, say this prayer. (Put it in your own words and *mean* it.)

> Dear God,
> I want to know You better. I believe that You have a lot to teach me about Yourself and about myself. Let me know what I need to know.
> And please help me as I raise my child[ren]. I especially need help in _____ [fill in with a specific need for that day].
> Thank you for listening. Amen.

2. Listen to Him. Each day for the next week, read a few verses in the Bible. Here are our suggestions:

Day 1—Psalm 23

Day 2— Ephesians 4:1–6, 25–32

Day 3—1 Corinthians 13

Day 4—James 1

Day 5—Matthew 6:25–34; 7:1–12

Day 6—John 3:1–21

Day 7—John 4:1–42

3. Talk to a pastor or a Christian who seems to know God well. Ask for his or her advice. If you would like additional material on how to be a Christian, call us at the Fresh Start office (1-800-882-2799).

	Day 1	Day 2	Day 3	Day 4	Day 5	Day 6	Day 7
Talk to God (What did you pray for?)							
Listen to Him (What did you read?)							

Talk to someone
  (Whom? _____)

Becoming a better parent can overwhelm you. Ask
God for help, even if you've never prayed before.
You need a miracle, in your life, in your home.
God can empower you.

— 5 —

The Overburdened Parent

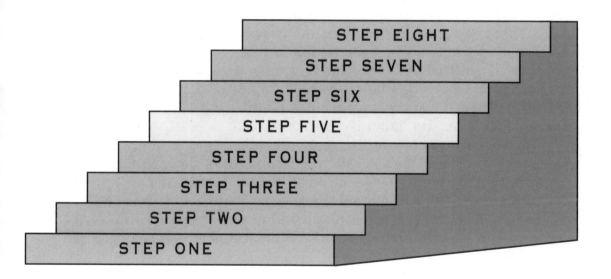

STEP FIVE

Set goals and take practical measures to improve the areas of life that burden you the most.

Jesus once said, "Come to Me, all you who labor and are heavy laden, and I will give you rest" (Matt. 11:28). I am convinced that this verse should be inscribed over the doorways of single-parent homes. Everyone who has to rear a child alone carries tremendous physical, emotional, spiritual, and financial concerns: "Are we still a family?" "If so, can we make this family work?" "How am I going to pay the bills?" "Where is God when we need Him?" And "How can I live through one more day like this?"

I have selected four of the most difficult issues a single parent faces. The core issue, however, in overcoming any of these hardships is found in your attitude. No person, no amount of money, and no job can rescue you from your situation if you have an attitude of failure and/or bitterness. In contrast, if you can take full responsibility for your own recovery and your personal growth, you must embrace an attitude of forgiveness.

FINANCIAL PRESSURES

Of all the problems single parents face, finances are probably mentioned the most and yet are the most difficult to address. Both moms and dads feel financial pressures, but studies show that men have more earning power and regain their financial loss more quickly.

Women have a harder adjustment for a variety of reasons. They may not have been working and must now seek employment—the embarrassment of an entry-level job or (worse) public assistance. Typically, the earning power for women is below that of men. Women make, on an average, less than $15,000 a year. From this they must subtract the expense of day care.

With income decreased considerably (about 76 percent within the first year), single mothers experience the added stress of trying to balance the budget. Frequently, little money is left for entertainment or pleasure. House repairs and auto maintenance are a struggle, since there is little money to have things done and not enough knowledge to do them yourself. The expectation of child-support payment from the ex-spouse is often shattered—approximately 50 percent of child support is never paid.

These financial burdens of the single parent suggest the need for practical guidelines for making some slow and steady progress. Here are some ideas for building for a more financially secure future.

Step One: Set Up a Budget

It has been said that people don't plan to fail, they just fail to plan. In the case of single-parent finances, set up a budget system for yourself that forces you to save a little for the future.

If you are like most single parents, you need to cut out all "extras" right away and focus on the necessities for you and your children. Sit down and set up a plan for you and your children.

Step Two: Stick to Your Plan, Despite Great Sacrifice

You will realize quickly that surviving financially requires difficult choices. You may need to get rid of credit cards, trade in your car, or sell your home and move to an apartment. Hopefully, the sacrifices will only be temporary.

One of the simplest plans for sticking to a budget is to place your monthly allocations into envelopes marked "food," "car," "clothes," and so on. Then you know exactly what you can spend each month in each category. When the envelope is empty, you know you have spent your limit. In the event of an emergency, you may have to dip into savings or borrow from another envelope to pay this bill.

Use credit cards only when you know that you will have the money to pay the bill *in full* at the end of the month. If debt is over 10 percent of your income, excluding mortgage, you're fighting a losing battle and you're going to need help.

Step Three: Get Help Wherever You Can

Pride can keep us from asking for help. If you are a single parent and make about $15,000 annually, then you need to swallow your pride and get some help. This help can take several forms. It doesn't have to mean public assistance or asking for money, but you need to be willing to take those steps if necessary. (The number of children receiving food stamps increases from 10 percent before divorce to 27 percent after divorce.)

Help comes in many forms, but most commonly comes from your family. Many single parents find that they have to move back home for a period of time or use family members for child care. Other forms of help come from your ex-spouse, who should be paying regular child support (if not, contact a lawyer), and may have to support you for a period of time with alimony. If you receive alimony for a period of time, use that time to gain training in a field that will allow you to make more than the average for single parents.

You can gain help from the church and other caring friends. Friends and agencies can provide financial counseling, child-care help, and maintenance assistance on the house and car. If your church does not presently offer this type of assistance, go to your church leaders and make a proposal on behalf of all the single parents in your congregation.

SAMPLE BUDGET

EXAMPLE #1: AVERAGE INCOME FOR SINGLE MOM

GROSS INCOME	= $15,000/yr	$1250/month
Taxes	= about 10%	125/month
Church/Charity	= about 10%	125/month
	Net Spendable Income =	$1000/month
Housing	= 30 to 40%	400/month
Utilities	= 10 to 15%	150/month
Food	= about 15%	150/month
Automobile	= about 10%	125/month
Insurance	= about 5%	50/month
Clothes	= 5%	50/month
Entertainment	= 5%	50/month
Savings	= whatever you can	25/month

BALANCED BUDGET $1250/MONTH

Earned Income Credit

If you earn under $20,000 a year, use the "earned income credit" on your Federal Income Taxes. Consult an IRS advisor if you have questions.

A close look at this proposed budget shows some things that seem unrealistic or missing. Make up your own budget to reflect *your* needs.

If you are only making about $15,000 a year, you are going to need some help.

Housing. Ideally, you should only be spending about 30 percent in this category, but if you are making a minimal salary and live in a fairly nice area, you may need to spend more to get decent housing. If so, you are going to have to make sacrifices in other areas such as transportation, clothing, and entertainment. If your housing is costing you more than 40 percent, you need to look at other options for you and your children. You may need to consider moving in with another family, into public housing, or with family or friends.

Utilities. Conserve as much as possible. This area includes electricity, phone, water, gas, and oil. If you have a house, all of these will be your responsibility. Even though a house is usually a better investment, if you are earning a minimal salary, an apartment may be your best choice now.

Food. With a family, 15 percent of your income may seem like an impossible goal for your food allotment. If you have a large family, consider public assistance, help from the church, or other creative ways of feeding your children. This budget will require that we get appropriate child support payments, that we shop for bargains, use coupons, buy generic brands, and cut out junk foods.

Transportation. This category can require 10–15 percent of your income depending on the type of car you drive. A general rule of thumb is that the least expensive car to own is the one you have. In other words, if your car is running, don't trade it in on a new one. Certainly there are exceptions to this rule, but keep in mind that while the car industry is trying to convince you that you need a new car, practically speaking this is not true. If at all possible, you need a car that is debt-free. If you need to downgrade (sell an expensive car to eliminate the payment) in order to meet your budget, ask if persons in your church, or friends or family members have a car they could give to you or donate to the church. If people are aware of your need, they might be willing to donate the car to the church for the tax write-off. Of course, you should have someone who is mechanically minded look over the car before you take it. You don't want to inherit someone else's headache or get something that would be unsafe for your children.

Insurance. You will have to decide which insurance you need. Do this with a *neutral* advisor or a trusted friend.

House and automobile insurance are necessities and are included in your housing and transportation budgets. Health insurance is a must. You need a job that includes health insurance for you and your children. Or ask your ex-spouse to include the children in his/her insurance policy. That way you only need health coverage for yourself. If none of these options is a possibility, look into Medicaid benefits.

Life insurance and disability insurance are nice options but are less of a priority. Again, a *neutral* advisor or trusted friend would be the best one to help you sort through your options.

Clothes. Allowing only 5 percent for clothing will take some creative shopping, and some help from others. Most of us have much more than we ever need and probably have outfits that we have worn only once or twice and then put aside. That is why we have thrift shops filled with good clothing. My own church has a "sharing room" filled with name-brand clothing that is in great shape. Single parents in our church feel free to discreetly take whatever they want from the supply of clothes. If your church has nothing of this nature, then you could be instrumental in starting a church clothing room. I find that people feel *much* better when they can give clothes to others rather than throw them away.

Stretch your clothing allowance by finding a friend the same size as you, or who has children of about the same age, who will share.

Entertainment. It is important that you plan to spend at least 5 percent of your income for a night out, an occasional singles' retreat, or something just for you. This area is critical to your sanity and the sanity of your children.

Savings. Savings can also take several forms. You need a fund for emergencies and an untouchable fund designated for your children's education or your retirement. The more you can put into savings the better. It is important that you save at least *something*. Don't be afraid to ask for help in investing.

Child Care. Forty percent of single parents pay some type of child care. You may need to allocate 10 percent of your budget for this need, but as you can see in the sample budget, there may be nothing available. That may require concessions in other areas in order to pay for your children's care. It would be best if you can find someone to help you in this area, or share the task with a group of single parents.

EXAMPLE #2: INCOME OF $30,000/YEAR

GROSS INCOME	= $30,000/yr	$2500/month
Taxes	= about 20%	500/month
Church/Charity	= about 10%	250/month
	Net Spendable Income =	$1750/month
Housing	= 30 to 40%	525/month
Utilities	= 10 to 15%	175/month
Food	= about 15%	250/month
Automobile	= about 10%	175/month
Insurance	= about 5%	90/month
Clothes	= 10%	175/month
Entertainment	= 5%	90/month
Child Care	= 10%	175/month
Savings	= whatever you can	95 month

BALANCED BUDGET $2500/MONTH

This second budget gives you a little more for living expenses, food, and clothes. It even has an allotment for child care. Get help in whatever area you can to provide more money for savings. Notice that the more you make, the more taxes you pay.

It is critical that you budget your funds; that you stick to your budget; and that you get help from friends and family. Help comes in many forms, but it is important that you speak up about your specific needs. As the New Testament says, "You do not have because you do not ask" (James 4:2).

Fill out a budget for you and your family.

GROSS INCOME		_____/year	_____/month
Taxes	10-30%		_____/month
Church/Charity	10%		_____/month
Spendable Income			_____/month
Housing	30-40%		_____/month
Utilities	10%		_____/month
Food	15%		_____/month
Automobile	10%		_____/month
Clothes	10%		_____/month
Insurance	?		_____/month
Child Care	?		_____/month
Entertainment	?		_____/month
Savings	?		_____/month

❶ You may want to double-check by looking over receipts, checkbook entries, and so on. How close to this budget have you been living? Do you need to adjust certain areas on the budget to be more realistic? (If so, do that now.)

Once you have written in the numbers for a realistic budget, look at your percentages and see if they are within an acceptable range. If

HOW TO LIVE ON LESS

Minor cuts	Major cuts	Help
Yard sales	Move to apt.	Church
Thrift shops	Trade in hot car	Ex
Cheaper food	Sell, pawn luxury	Family
Eat in	items	Friends
Less entertainment	Discard credit cards	Single-parents'
Cut subscriptions,		network
cable TV,		Welfare
gadgets, impulse		
buying		

not, do you need to cut back further in some areas to make your overall budget work and still have some savings?

❷ Compared to the way you *have been* spending, what areas will need to be significantly cut back in order to meet this new budget? _____

_____

_____

❸ What do you think will be the hardest cutback, "the unkindest cut of all"? _____

_____

Finances can be a major burden for the single parent.
Smart budgeting and simplified living is essential.

Action Point: If you need to do some work on staying within your budget, write what you need to do here in the form of a goal and again in Appendix A. _____

_____

_____

NOT ENOUGH TIME

After finances, *time* is the next area of concern. This is primarily true of the custodial parent, but is also a challenge for the noncustodial parent. As with finances, there is not enough time to go around. You can find ways to improve your time management. Here are some practical steps for you to take.

Step One: Determine Your Priorities

Tom Landry of the Dallas Cowboys was one of the *winning*est coaches in football. Addressing a group of college students, he was asked about the secret of his success. He responded, "In 1958, I did something everyone who has been successful must do; I determined my priorities for life—God, family, and then football."

As you list all your jobs and responsibilities that you have, try to determine your priorities. Probably your children, your spiritual life, yourself, and your job would be high on your priority list. What other responsibilities do you now have that you find you just can't keep up with? You will have to give up some of these activities. To make the right choices, consider how each activity matches your overall priorities.

A good example would be Molly's situation. Being the single parent of three children, she found she didn't have the time or energy for all of her obligations. She had a membership at the local YMCA, but with her new life-style, she had little time to go. She was about to cancel her membership when she took the time to list her priorities. Her children and her own well-being were high on her priority list. She decided to renew her membership and cut out some other activities. The visits to the YMCA were great times for her and her children to play together. At the same time, she benefited from the aerobics classes.

Step Two: Learn to Say No

I am still learning how to say no. If someone has a need and wants me to meet it, I have a terrible time turning them down. But if I am to stick to my priorities in life, sometimes I have to. I can't do it all.

Many others share my problem—perhaps you do, too. "People pleasing" is the culprit. We want to please others, even at the expense of our own well-being. People-pleasing can be particularly strong when we have been through a significant rejection, such as divorce—since everything within us cries out for acceptance. We long for the approval of our children, our family, our church friends, or our coworkers. However, we still need to evaluate each request according to our stated priorities.

Another person you might need to learn to say no to is yourself. I have talked with many single parents who have made statements similar to this:

I like a neat and orderly home. I like my children to be on a regular schedule, and I like to have everything in its place at the end of the day. That is, until my divorce. Now I've learned to go with the flow a little bit. To tolerate a little more chaos, and to expect that, at any given time, it is most likely that one room in the house is an absolute mess. But that's okay, because I've learned that my sanity is more important than order.

That's a priority statement—"My sanity is more important than order." Many of us have similar compulsions. We must examine our choices in light of our priorities. Sometimes you must "just say no" to your own desires or compulsions in order to get on with what's really important.

——— MAKE IT YOUR OWN ———

❶ What are your priorities? How are you investing your time? List them in the space below. I've given some suggested responses, but you may have other ideas. List what's really true for you.

1. _____
2. _____
3. _____
4. _____
5. _____

Suggestions: Serving God; rearing children properly; advancing in career; dating; making enough money to support family; doing good to others; developing my relationship with God; showing love to my kids; proving to my ex that I can make it on my own; enjoying myself.

❷ Now look over your list. Is there anything you want to change? Are your priorities where you think they should be? Make any adjustments you think necessary.

3 Can you remember the five things you've recently been asked to do? Did you say yes or no? These may be simple things, like taking your kids to the zoo, or major things, like directing a school play. Try to include at least one major commitment and at least two requests that did not come from your children.

1. _____
2. _____
3. _____
4. _____
5. _____

Go back over these five requests and write "Yes" or "No" in the left margin, depending on how you responded to the request.

Now consider how each of these tied in with your priorities. If one of these requests would help you accomplish one of the five priorities you listed earlier, write the number of that priority in the margin (next to the Yes or No) and circle it.

Ideally, you should have numbers next to your yesses and not next to your noes. As you examine these requests in light of your priorities, are these yesses you should have said no to and noes you should have said yes to?

4 How can you use your priorities to make better decisions in the future? _____

_____

_____

Step Three: Learn How to Delegate

You *can't* do it all yourself. We need to learn to ask for help and then to graciously accept it.

Think about all the roles that you fulfilled while you were married. Now think about all the roles your spouse fulfilled. (I mean on his/her good days.) With your spouse now out of the picture, how can you expect to do it all yourself?

Once you have set your priorities and have started saying no to any responsibilities that don't fit into your most urgent needs, those tasks that still remain must get done anyway—like cutting the grass, walking the dog, taking out the trash, maintaining the car. The list goes on and on. The art of delegation comes in handy here.

The children are the first persons who come to mind when it comes to delegation. They can be a big help. But they must be allowed to remain children.

The kids are not enough! You are going to need other people in your life—other adults. For example, your children cannot become your counselor or your best friend. They probably can't fix the car, or help you make wise investments. For many tasks you will need a support network of people you can count on. Begin thinking now of people you would like to include in this list of trusted friends or counselors you can call on for help.

—— MAKE IT YOUR OWN ——

❶ What roles did your former spouse fulfill for you? Check all that apply.

☐ advisor	☐ housekeeper
☐ bill payer	☐ investor
☐ bookkeeper	☐ landscaper
☐ cook	☐ launderer
☐ counselor	☐ lover
☐ decorator	☐ mechanic
☐ friend	☐ painter
☐ gardener	☐ provider

❷ What additional roles did your former mate play? _____

_____

_____

Now look back over the roles you checked or listed. Rather than take all of those roles on yourself, why not delegate? Next to each of the roles you checked or listed, try to think of someone who would help you accomplish that task.

Look over the list above and write the initials of the people you might ask to fill those roles (or who are already filling those roles). Remember that not all those roles need to be filled.

──────── **MAKE IT YOUR OWN** ────────

❶ In the space below, jot the name(s) of your child(ren) and then list the additional tasks and roles they now have in the home. List the roles and tasks they are actually assuming.

Child	*Task*
_____	_____
_____	_____
_____	_____
_____	_____

❷ Now go back over this list. Are any of the tasks or responsibilities too great for them to take on? Are any roles inappropriate for their age? If so, circle these.

❸ Are there some tasks they *could* do, but they're not choosing to? Put a box around these on the list you just made.

❹ Are there other tasks you need them to take on (assuming that these are appropriate to their age and abilities)? If so, write these in and underline them.

Action Point: Meet with your kid(s) about the division of responsibilities in your home. Use this opportunity to hear their perspectives on the roles they are filling. Be sure to do the following:

▶ Go through the circled items on your list and explain that you do not expect them to do these things anymore. Be sure that this does not come across as a put-down, but that your concern and love shows through.

▶ Go through the boxed items on your list and talk about how your child(ren) could do these things better. You may need to give instructions or explain your expectations.

▶ Introduce your child(ren) to the underlined items on your list. Ask them if they'd like to help you out in these ways. Make sure they know how to do these things and what is expected of them.

Make this family meeting one of your goals and be sure to write it in Appendix A and to check it off your list once you have accomplished a successful family meeting.

Time is a critical issue for the single parent. Determine your priorities, say no to obligations that don't fit into those priorities, and build a support network that can help you manage some specific tasks.

FEELINGS OF FAILURE

Anyone who goes through the breakup of a significant relationship is going to feel the failure. This experience can lead us to a new determination to make it on our own, or it can lead us to a view of the world as hostile and negative.

Negative experiences—particularly when they are significant—can lead us to negative thinking, or "dysfunctional thinking." If you grew up in a difficult home situation, then you are quite familiar with this line of reasoning. And it is likely that the death or divorce of your spouse is only reinforcing these cognitive traps for you and your children.

Effects On Our Thinking: Cognitive Traps

▶ *All-or-Nothing Thinking.* When the whole house is clean but the children mess up one room, you conclude that the house is a disaster or that you are a terrible housekeeper. When one of your children gets into trouble, you feel like a failure as a parent.

▶ *Overgeneralization.* You frequently use words like *never* and *always*, especially when dealing with your children or your former spouse. You say, "You're always late." "You never support me." "You never listen to me; you're always too busy doing other things." Such statements are not true, but we revert to them in times of tension, frustration, and excitement.

▶ *Mental Filter.* One word of criticism wipes out all the positive comments you have received. You tend to be particularly sensitive about your parenting and relational skills because those are the skills that have been attacked most in your divorce. You filter out all your positive accomplishments and accentuate your failures at marriage, homemaking, career, or parenting. All single parents have to deal with such failures, but you cannot define yourself by your shortcomings.

▶ *Discounting the Positive.* The fact that you work hard, do a lot, and have survived a great deal of pain is discounted. You conclude, "That doesn't count." "Anyone would have done the same." "I'm only surviving." Those words do not give you credit for the many positive things you do.

▶ *Jumping to Conclusions.* You conclude that others do not respect you, that the church has rejected you, or that you should not bother trying because you will only fail. Your conclusions are usually negative because your thinking has been twisted by your divorce. The experience of failure can cause you to conclude that whatever you do will fail. Negative thinking can become a self-perpetuating cycle.

▶ *Magnification and Minimization.* As single parent, there is no question that you have more than your share of problems. But this form of thinking causes you to magnify your problems. You feel your kids are a mess and will never amount to anything. You fear your bills will never be paid and you will lose everything. You're convinced that your former spouse has absolutely no good qualities. At the same time, you minimize the good things that happen. You get a promotion at work and conclude that you were just lucky. Your former spouse does something nice for you, so you assume that "he must be up to something." Your children do well in school, and you wonder how long it will last.

▶ *Emotional Reasoning.* As a single parent you can be very emotional—with good reason. You are vulnerable and, at times, physically exhausted. That can cause you to "think with your feelings." In other words, you tell yourself that you feel lousy today, your situation is hopeless. When you feel better, things will be okay. Emotional reasoning can cause the single parenting experience to feel like an emotional roller coaster and can cause you to be unstable in your relationships with others.

▶ *"Should" Statements.* Some people try to live their lives according to "should" and "ought" statements. That is a trap because you can never measure up. No matter how much you do, you tell yourself that you really *should* do more. Can you ever really fulfill the following statements?

"I ought to listen to my children more.

"I should spend more time helping my children with their schoolwork."

"I need to spend more time in Bible study and prayer."

"I should pay more attention to my work."

"I should keep the house cleaner."

"I ought to be more organized." If you've made such statements, you are setting yourself up for failure and a guilt trap—a common occurrence among single parents.

▶ *Labeling.* This is a more extreme form of all-or-nothing thinking and magnification of the negative. Instead of saying, "I made a mistake," you label yourself a loser. You say, "I'm an idiot," because you forget an appointment. This kind of thinking corresponds to a poor self-image and, unfortunately, is passed on to your children because you can't help but model it to them.

▶ *Personalization and Blame.* There has been plenty that has gone wrong in your life, but not all of it is your fault. This form of thinking, however, leads you to take everything onto your shoulders. You say, "If I'd only been a better wife, my husband would not have run off like he did." "My children are doing poorly in school. I must be a terrible mother." "Others are rude to me because I bring it on myself." "I really shouldn't take that bad chicken back to the store because I know I'm a bad shopper."

(Adapted from *The Feeling Good Handbook,* by David Burns)

These patterns of thinking can debilitate us. They can prevent us from moving on with our lives in healthy ways. If we persist in these ways of thinking, we model them for our children. We need to recognize these tendencies in ourselves and fight them. *For the sake of your children,* find new, more positive ways of thinking. I use the mental image of a fish swimming upstream as I try to fight these thoughts in my own life. The stream is the natural tendency to put yourself down or to dwell on the negative. We need to swim against this current. Become aware of your thought patterns, and correct them where necessary. If we stop disciplining our thoughts like this, we will just float downstream with that negative current. But swimming upstream will build strength, character, and a better life for our children.

> We reinforce feelings of failure by negative thought patterns. We must learn to recognize these patterns as they affect our thoughts, and we must fight against them.

———— MAKE IT YOUR OWN ————

Some psychologists promote the concept of "self-talk." This is basically what it sounds like, talking to yourself, telling yourself what you need to hear. It is a helpful strategy in combating negative thought patterns.

For each of the ten patterns I listed earlier, I'll offer a typical *negative* statement, and then an underlying attitude. See if you can come up with a *positive* statement to counteract the negative.

1. *All-or-nothing.*

    Statement: "I see those A's, but how could you get a D in math?"
    Underlying attitude: "If it's not perfect, it's not good enough."

    Positive statement: _____

_____

_____

2. *Overgeneralization*

    Statement: "All of these stoplights are turning red as I approach. It's like they know I'm coming."
    Underlying attitude: "Everything goes wrong for me."

    Positive statement: _____

_____

_____

3. *Mental filter*

    Statement: "My boss wants me to redo the report with more updated figures. He must have hated it."
    Underlying attitude: "When people criticize anything about me, they must hate me."

    Positive statement: _____

_____

_____

4. *Discounting the positive*

    Statement: "I know they said they were glad to see me, but they sure seemed happy when I got up to leave."
    Underlying attitude: "People don't mean the good things they say about me."

    Positive statement: _____

_____

_____

5. Jumping to conclusions

Statement: "Why go to that singles group? I won't meet anyone interesting."

Underlying attitude: "Nothing good will happen, so why bother?"

Positive statement: _____

_____

_____

6. Magnification

Statement: "Sure, I have a fun personality, but I also have a huge nose. People never see past it. Seriously!"

Underlying attitude: "My flaws are far greater than my attributes."

Positive statement: _____

_____

_____

7. Emotional reasoning

Statement: "I felt so nervous. I know I did a lousy job with that presentation."

Underlying attitude: "Reality is whatever I feel."

Positive statement: _____

_____

_____

8. Should statements

Statement: "I should be more outgoing and meet more people."

Underlying attitude: "There are many things that I ought to do that I'm not doing. I'm just not good enough to do them all."

Positive statement: _____

_____

_____

9. Labeling

Statement: "I botched that assignment. I'm just a second-rate worker."

Underlying attitude: "I am fundamentally flawed, and therefore I don't succeed."

Positive statement: _____

_____

_____

BILL OF RIGHTS FOR SINGLE PARENTS

1. You have the right to set aside time for yourself, your hobbies, your interests, and your social life.

2. You have the right to put the children to bed early so that you can have some time to yourself.

3. You have the right to attend a retreat or weekend away once in a while for your own mental health.

4. You have the right to say no to your children when they are too demanding or when they request unnecessary things.

5. You have the right to get baby-sitters for your children so that you can go out with your friends.

6. You have the right to insist that your ex-spouse maintain a regular and consistent visitation schedule.

7. You have the right to your own privacy.

8. You have the right to pursue your dream, whether it involves going back to school, changing careers, or saving for a special trip.

[adapted from *Better Homes and Gardens*, April 1992, p. 33]

10. Personalization and blame

Statement: "If I were a better parent, my kids would be doing better in school."

Underlying attitude: "Everything that goes wrong is my fault."

Positive statement: _____

_____

_____

————— **MAKE IT YOUR OWN** —————

❶ As you look over your list of rights, which do you feel you have neglected? _____

_____

_____

_____

❷ Which of the rights have you insisted on? _____

_____

_____

_____

❸ Do you have a dream or ambition that you need to pursue? Write it here—and include when you think you might be able to accomplish it. _____

_____

_____

_____

_____

FEELINGS OF ISOLATION

Scoti Springfield Domeij, a single mom in Southern California, described her feelings of isolation:

> The pain never ends. Each day, I battle physical and mental exhaustion from the incredible financial stress, the pain of loneliness, and the constant struggles with my ex-spouse. At first, I would cry all day and all night long. The only way I could get a grip on my emotions was to reach for the Bible and read Psalms aloud or sing praise songs. I cried when I woke up, I cried after dropping off the children at the babysitter, I cried on the way to work. I would set a goal to accomplish before my break, then I would go cry in the bathroom. It went like this all day long.
>
> Some days my heart is not in my work because I want to be home with my children. They are growing up so quickly, and I am missing everything. I have no memories to cherish. My baby said his first word the other day, and the babysitter was sweet enough to tell me about it.
>
> I struggle to be a family, to have time together with my kids, but all my body wants to do is sleep. I am physically and emotionally too exhausted to drag myself from bed to go to my job each day. On the way to the babysitter in the morning, my left hand firmly grips the steering wheel while the right hand inserts bits of grapes, cubed cheese, or cut-up hot dogs into eager mouths.
>
> After a long day at work, I eagerly look forward to looking into the beautiful blue eyes of my two precious children. But after our loving reunion, my boys are hungry and complaining. After I fix dinner, get the laundry out, clean up, start baths, and have a short devotional time, I have little strength left. Several times, I've awakened in the middle of the night to find myself slumped in the middle of the living room floor.
>
> Abandoned, I am terrified of the future. The realization that I am alone and responsible for my small boys is overwhelming.
>
> —From "A Single Parent Shares the Pain," *Focus*, January 1989

Did this writer sound like she was describing your life? She was able to describe the isolation we all have felt after being left alone with so many responsibilities. As your family seems to disintegrate, it is not uncommon for former friends to pull away as well. The prior support systems fracture, and questions of self-esteem and self-worth arise: "Am I important to anyone?" "Does anyone really care about me?"

Your children are also isolated if a move has occurred. They leave familiar places and friends behind. New and strange responsibilities, coupled with feelings of loss, anger, and depression, further separate them from their peers.

Against these emotions, single parents strive to prove that their family is nevertheless okay. Offers of help are turned down due to pride or fear. No parent wants to admit, "I can't handle things." Thus the

HANDLING THE HOLIDAYS

1. Plan your holidays well in advance, and go over the plans with your children.

2. Talk with your ex-spouse well before the holiday in order to arrange visitation around the holidays. Working through this in advance will do much to make the holidays more enjoyable for you and your children. Once you've decided on a schedule, sit down with your children and tell them what to expect. Be upbeat and supportive. They may not ask you questions in advance, but you can bet that they will be thinking about it regularly.

3. Watch your expectation level. Don't expect too much. If you expect a joyous time, you have a greater likelihood of disappointment and post-holiday depression. On the other hand, expecting a terrible holiday can turn into a self-fulfilling prophecy. Approach each event with a little anticipation but be realistic about the difficulties you face.

4. Don't try to duplicate all of the old traditions. This will only remind your children of the fact that the other parent is not present. Be consistent and traditional but include a few new special events that will grow into new traditions and a new life-style.

overwhelming feeling among single parents is that they are all alone. There is no significant other person to share the joys, no one to share the responsibilities, and no one to share the discipline.

Because of this isolation, it is critical that we make a conscious effort to develop new friendships and a new support group. We must take full responsibility for our own recovery and begin moving forward into a new lifestyle.

Your moving on with your life is also of critical importance to your children. They need exposure to complete families to understand the relationships displayed in an intact family. Since most single parents are mothers, it is important to provide strong male role models if you are to break the cycle of divorce and dysfunction for your children.

To address this need, approach families that you consider healthy and ask them about helping you with your children. Extended family members such as uncles or grandparents can be helpful. Consider other trusted friends or church families for family outings, camping trips, and ball games. (Traditional family times; such as holidays, birthdays, and anniversaries, are generally lonely times for single-parent families. Plan them well in advance, so that you don't find yourself "celebrating" these moments alone.)

> Feelings of isolation are common among single parents. They can overwhelm you. Make time to be with others who understand you. Together, you can combat these lonely feelings.

─────── **MAKE IT YOUR OWN** ───────

❶ On a scale of 1 to 10, how isolated do you feel right now (10 is most)? _____

❷ When in the last year have you felt most alone? Describe the circumstances. _____

_____

_____

❸ What do you do when you feel lonely? _____

_____

_____

❹ What people or circumstances (place, activity, group) help to get you out of your feelings of isolation? _____

_____

_____

_____

Action Point: Can you make a special contact with some group or family to "adopt" you and give you the support you need to shake these feelings of isolation?

Some churches and communities have single-parent groups or divorce recovery groups that may help. Other "singles" groups function as "families." Look for a group where people truly care for you and are building true friendships. Invest yourself in that group.

What we're talking about here is "family." Your own single-parent family needs the support of a larger "family"—emotionally, relationally, practically, materially. Perhaps your own family of origin will provide the support you need.

Maybe you can "adopt" a family in your church or community. Be straightforward in discussing this. Say, "My kids need help, and I need help. We need a good family model to watch and to share some experiences with. Frankly, I need someone to watch the kids occasionally while I do other things. On the other hand, I can watch your kids sometimes while you go out. We don't want to abuse the friendship in any way, but we are pretty needy right now. Could we agree to get our families together every week or two?"

You may even wish to be more specific in details of such an arrangement. "If my kids can hang out at your place in the afternoons until I get home, I'll take yours out with mine on Wednesdays and Fridays."

You may be rejected. You're asking for a substantial commitment. If so, look for another loving family and try again. (And you may want to reconsider some details of the arrangement.)

——— MAKE IT YOUR OWN ———

❶ What individuals, families, or groups can you connect with to get the support you need?

GROUPS: (singles group, recovery group, church group) _____

_____

INDIVIDUALS: (role model for kids, "best friend" for you) _____

_____

FAMILIES: (an "adoptive" family, role models) _____

_____

❷ Whom could you contact *this week* to get this support going? ___

_____

If you can set a goal for either an individual, group, or family you intend to contact for emotional support, write that goal on page 237 (Appendix A) for future reference.

— 6 —

The Overburdened Child

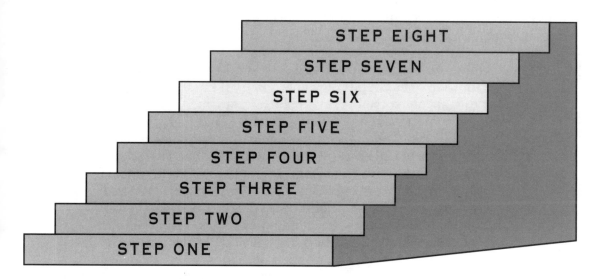

STEP SIX

Set goals and take practical measures to improve life for your children.

Tony Campolo, Professor of Sociology at Eastern College, author, and frequent guest lecturer, told the following story in the Fresh Start book *My Parents Got a Divorce:*

I was once a host for one of those early morning television talk shows. I interviewed all kinds of people about all kinds of things in an effort to make for some interesting broadcast time.

One morning I was interviewing a couple that had written a book on "creative divorce." They spent most of our hour together trying to convince me and the TV audience that they had found the secret as to how to dissolve a marriage without acrimony or rancor.

It was all so lighthearted and fluffy. They giggled and joked and tried very hard to make the point that they were really better friends now that they were divorced than they had ever been before.

They explained how their marriage had stifled their creativity and individuality. They made rambling speeches sprinkled with the phrases that we all have learned to expect from those who are high on the Human Potential Movement. In the course of the interview they explained how the divorce had freed each of them up "to find their true selves" and "to actualize their respective personhoods." They talked about the ways that they "realized who they really were through the painful process of self-definition that goes on during the struggles of divorce." It was the kind of chatter that fills an hour of broadcast time and leaves the viewer wondering why he or she bothered to watch.

I was not the least bit judgmental until the last few minutes of the show. "After all," I thought to myself, "if that's what they want to do—it's a free country."

My easy-going acceptance of these guests, who seemed to deal with marriage and divorce in such a cavalier manner, quickly ended when they happened to mention their children. When I found out that children had been caught in the mess, I could not help but seriously zero in on them and ask as pointedly as I knew how, "How does all of this affect your kids?"

The two of them tried to explain that, while it was difficult at first, the children had learned to accept the divorce and were now "perfectly adjusted." The woman talked of all the "love" that her children were receiving at their day-care center. She smiled and said that it was undoubtedly more healthy for them to be spending eight hours each day with "professionals" who know how to raise children than to be "stuck" with their mother all day.

Dad tried to convince me that although he only sees the children every other weekend, he has a close and healthy relationship with them.

There was no need for me to strip bare their arguments and declarations. The phoniness of it all was too obvious to deserve comment. I just let them go on and on making their claims, that "if handled properly, divorce has no adverse effects on children."

When the show ended, one of the cameramen muttered to me under his breath, "Who do they think they are kidding besides themselves?"

Divorce is a disaster! Divorce is so disruptive in the lives of children that it is cited as a major factor leading to drug use, premarital sex, and delinquency.

This is not to say that such results necessarily flow from a divorce. It is only to point out that such behavioral patterns are more likely to be evident among children of divorced couples than among children from intact families. The research indicates that the only thing that is worse than divorce is desertion. In the latter case, the pain and guilt often proves too much for the children to bear.

There are a wide range of painful reactions to divorce. Some children blame themselves for what has happened, thinking that "if they had been better children then Daddy would not have left." Others are consumed with seething anger and spend their lives working out their aggression on innocent people who just happen to be available.

But what is saddest of all is that among the children of the divorced there is a strong likelihood that they will repeat the same mistakes as their parents. The children of divorced couples are much more likely than the children from intact families to experience marital disruption and to have severe problems in relating to the opposite sex. Indeed there is ample evidence to support the biblical declaration, "The sins of the fathers shall be upon the children and the children's children." Divorce has far-reaching consequences for the children.

The Troubled Children of Single-Parent Families

	Unmarried Mothers	Divorced Mothers	Both Parents
Children in poverty	63%	34%	11%
Repeated a grade in school	33%	23%	13%
Suspended or expelled	17%	11%	5%
On welfare for more than 10 years	39%	14%	N/A
Children in juvenile detention	——56%——		28%

Copyright June 8, 1992, *U.S. News & World Report*

Divorce *is* a burden on our children, and growing up in a single-parent family can overburden our children with chores, responsibilities, and the loss of innocence. In this chapter we will examine some of the common burdens that we as single parents must guard against. Breaking the cycle of divorce and dysfunction with our children requires that we recognize these burdens and work at lessening the unhealthy patterns of parenting.

SCHIZOPHRENIC PARENTING

Billy is much like other ten-year-old boys except that he leads two lives. He lives with his mother from Monday to Thursday and then goes to his dad's from Friday to Sunday. His life in each home changes dramatically.

At his mom's, Billy has a regimented schedule, a list of chores, and strict instructions about his behavior while mom is at work. He must start his homework as soon as he gets home from school and then promptly at 5:00 P.M. set the table and begin to prepare the evening meal. His mother comes home by 6:00, finishes dinner, checks his homework, and then they work together on the evening chores such as cleaning and laundry. If time allows, he might watch some television.

When Billy is at his dad's, life is very different. He has no real schedule, and he hasn't figured out yet if there are any rules. They usually send out for fast food and eat it in front of the television. Billy has yet to wash a dish or make his bed while at his father's.

Where do you think Billy likes to be? While Billy likes the freedom and fun of dad's house, he now longs for a more consistent and secure life-style, such as he gets from his mother. The real issue is the burden such a diverse life-style places on a ten-year-old boy. Living two different lives is confusing to both children and adults. How will he determine his values, beliefs, and patterns of life? The Bible summarizes this dilemma best in James 1:8, speaking of the "double-minded man" who "is unstable in all his ways."

This schizophrenic style of parenting is disruptive to our children, and we as parents need to work at presenting a united front. As single parents you need to guard against exposing your children to conflicting life-styles.

How are you to respond, for instance, when your child asks, "Is it right for Daddy to be living with his girlfriend?" As a parent, this puts you in the uncomfortable position of either not dealing with the issue honestly or being critical of the other parent. Many parents would use the opportunity to blast the other parent's life-style, but a more responsible response would be, "No, it's not right for your father to live with his girlfriend, but he's still your father, and therefore you need to show him respect."

The best way to overcome the adverse effects on your children of being reared with conflicting values is for you and your former spouse to agree to coparent. You discuss together the setting of rules, boundaries, and ethics you want your children to live by. It is best if you can agree on these standards. Your children will pay the price of double standards.

─────── **MAKE IT YOUR OWN** ───────

If you are widowed or if your ex has no involvement with the children, double standards are not a problem. Move past these questions to the next section.

But if you do have to deal with visitation or shared custody, continue on.

❶ On a scale of 1 to 10, 1 being "very similar" and 10 being "very different," how different are the personal values of you and your ex?

very similar   very different

    1   2   3   4   5   6   7   8   9   10

❷ On the same scale, how different are your life-styles?

very similar   very different

    1   2   3   4   5   6   7   8   9   10

❸ On the same scale, how different are your rules for the kids?

very similar   very different

    1   2   3   4   5   6   7   8   9   10

❹ List five things the two of you agree on in child-rearing.

1. _____

2. _____

3. _____

4. _____

5. _____

❺ List five things you disagree on.

    1. _____

    2. _____

    3. _____

    4. _____

    5. _____

❻ Ask your child[ren] to list five things that are different about staying with mom and staying with dad.

    1. _____

    2. _____

    3. _____

    4. _____

    5. _____

❼ What is the most serious disagreement/difference? _____

_____

_____

❽ Can you compromise on this end and reach an agreement that would be healthy for the child[ren]? How would you start? _____

_____

_____

❾ If that one is too difficult, try this: What is the disagreement/ difference that is easiest to resolve? _____

_____

How would you go about resolving that? _____

_____

Action Point: If complete harmony is impossible, can you bend a bit *unilaterally* for the good of the children? Write at least one thing or attitude that you can change to create more harmony for your children. Write it here and in Appendix A.

_____

_____

_____

COPING WITH MAJOR CHANGES

Major disruptions to the family, such as a death or a broken relationship, produce changes to endure—changes in life-style, moods, and the way we relate to one another.

As a single parent you will move more often, change churches and school districts more often, and have more changes in your close circle of intimate friends than other families. As just one small indication of this, at Fresh Start we have a mailing list of about 5,000 single parents. Each year, we find that about a third of our single parents have moved. Consider the number of relationship changes that involves: changes of friends, neighbors, and classmates. And what about friends of the opposite sex? They come into our lives, into our children's lives, introduce us to a whole new circle of friends and family, and then one day they're gone. What does all this change do to our children?

Here is a list of some of the most stressful childhood events, according to David Elkind's book *The Hurried Child*.

Stress	Points	Your Child
Parent dies	100	_____
Parents divorce	73	_____
Parents separate	65	_____
Parent travels as part of job	63	_____
Close family member dies	63	_____
Personal illness or injury	53	_____

Stress	Points	Your Child
Parent remarries	50	_____
Parent fired from job	47	_____
Parents reconcile	45	_____
Mother goes to work	45	_____
Mother becomes pregnant	40	_____
School difficulties	39	_____
Birth of a sibling	39	_____
New teacher or new class	39	_____
Change in family finances	38	_____
Injury or illness of close friend	37	_____
Fight between siblings	35	_____
Threat of violence at school	31	_____
Theft of personal possessions	30	_____
Change in responsibilities at home	29	_____
Older sibling leaves home	29	_____
Trouble with grandparents	29	_____
A move	26	_____
Losing a pet	25	_____
Change to a new school	20	_____
Vacations with family	19	_____
Change in friends	18	_____
Change in family traditions	15	_____
Punishment for lying	11	_____

———— **M A K E   I T   Y O U R   O W N** ————

Look through this list, and determine how many points your children have accumulated. Write the appropriate number of points in the column at the right. If you're like most single parents, the stresses are extremely high.

Now go through the list again and consider, how many stresses were a direct result of your divorce or the death of your spouse. Put a *D* next to the point totals in each of these areas. (Naturally, the divorce itself qualities, so place a *D* there.) Total up the number of *D* points and write it here. _____

❶ Now, how many of these stressors resulted from choices you made? Put a *C* next to each of these.

❷ Go back through the *C* points. How many of those choices were inevitable or necessary? Put an *N* next to the *C* in each of these cases. Total up the *CN* points now. _____

❸ Now go back and total the points with just a *C*. Put that answer here _____

Every child will encounter a certain amount of stressors. *Your* child has an *additional* amount of stress—all those *D* points you counted up. That's probably a high percentage of the total stress points. But there's not much you can do about that now—except to look for *other* areas where you can minimize stress.

We'll find those in the *C* areas—stress-causing choices we've made. Some of these choices are necessary *(CN)*, as we've seen. But the total of *C* points indicate areas where you can work at keeping stress to a minimum.

KEEPING STRESS AT A MINIMUM

Here are a few ideas for keeping stress at a minimum.

Minimize Changes

Try to plan your moves to provide consistency. For example, move within the same school district, stay in the same church, or even delay a move for a year or more while your children make necessary adjustments.

Encourage a Relationship with Stable Family Members

If you have stable family members nearby—an uncle, aunt, grandparents—encourage their involvement with your children.

Sometimes these relationships can be the most stable thing in your children's lives, including their relationship with you. You may be too distracted with your own problems to be a stable support for your kids. Ask your family to step in, if they can be counted on to be a stable influence.

Minimize Involvement with Passing Relationships

Your dating relationships can be very transitory. Even if you consider a one-year relationship to be long-term, to your children this can be devastating. Think about it. Their father said he loved them and would never leave. But he did. Now there is a new man in your life, and he loves your children. You all spend time together. You might even get to know his whole family, and the children seem to be thrilled with the affection they are shown. But after a year or so, this man is also out of your life and your children never see him again. Repeat this process several times, and you can see why children experience significant stress, along with distorted views of a man's role in the family.

Minimize your children's contact with your dating relationships, their friends, and their family, until you are fairly certain that it is going to be a permanent relationship. That doesn't mean that you shouldn't do things together as a family with your dates. Weekend picnics, sporting events, and trips to the zoo can be fun for everyone, and your dates will need to at least get to know and hopefully like your children. However, be sure you make clear to your children the nature of the relationship. You could say, "Bill and I are friends. We are getting to know each other and we like each other a lot, but that doesn't mean he will always be a part of our lives."

Downplay the permanency of the relationship until you know a marriage is going to take place. Vacations together are out, extended trips to your friend's family for the holidays are a no-no, and I would even caution you against having your friend take the kids on outings alone. You must constantly think about the bonds your friend is building with your kids and how that will affect them if you break up. Get a family member or a friend who does not have a romantic interest in you to fill this role for your children.

Do Not Discuss Contingency Plans with Your Children

When you know that you are going to have to make a change, get everyone together for a family meeting. If the children can have a say in the decision, open it up for discussion. If there is no room for discussion, inform them as lovingly as possible. Otherwise, keep your dreams and schemes to yourself.

At times of financial crisis, don't overreact. It does not instill a sense of stability in your children. Get a handle on your emotional reactions.

———— MAKE IT YOUR OWN ————

Answer all that apply:

❶ What major changes do you see in the next year (a move, school change, etc.)? _____

_____

_____

❷ How can you minimize the impact of these changes (move closer, delay the move, etc.)? _____

_____

_____

❸ What family members could your kids be closer to, to provide some stability? _____

_____

_____

❹ If you are in a new romantic relationship, do you feel this person is too close to your kids, not close enough, or just right? _____

_____

_____

❺ What sort of things do you think it's all right to do as a family with this new person in your life? _____

_____

_____

❻ What sort of things might be too dangerous at this point in your relationship (possibly setting the children up for disappointment)?

_____

_____

❼ What contingency plans are you worried about presently that you don't need to share with the kids? _____

_____

_____

❽ At what point do you think you could share these things with the kids? _____

_____

_____

Any change of life-style or relationship places an emotional burden on children. You can minimize the effects of these changes with careful planning and forethought.

BEING OVERBURDENED WITH RESPONSIBILITIES

Darryl is a typical "latchkey" kid. He sees his father a few times a year because he lives 1,000 miles away. His mom is a nurse and works 10 to 12 hours per day. She dates two or three nights a week.

Darryl has three younger siblings he must help care for. In the morning he helps fix their breakfast, pack their books, and get them to the bus stop on time. Then he has his own school responsibilities and chores around the house, which include the lawn and minor repairs.

Darryl is home alone after school with his two brothers and sisters from about 4:00 till 6:00 P.M. They generally play in the neighborhood and fend for themselves until mom gets home after six and fixes their dinner. When questioned about his home life and his family, Darryl will respond with assurances of his ability to take care of himself and the fact that he doesn't need anyone. The truth is that he's a young boy who has shut out the pain by telling himself that he can make it on his own. He thinks he can live without love and support, but someday he will find out that we need love and security!

I encourage parents to push their children to become independent and self-reliant as early as possible. But we must balance this with our children's need to be children—not mature adults at the age of twelve. Yet single-parent families often push kids to grow up and take care of themselves. After all, it *would* be a big help!

In most homes, parents make decisions, provide structure, and model adulthood to their children. There is a hierarchy of parental leadership in the healthy family.

Yet the single-parent family has experienced a breakdown in the leadership structure. Many times parents turn to their children for the missing support. In this way we overburden our children.

Single-parent children as a rule *do* have more responsibilities than other children. But try not to overburden your children. Your son is *not* the man of the house; your daughter is *not* the lady of the house; neither fits the role of confidant or "best friend." Let them remain your children.

Bring in Responsible Babysitters

Most single parents have to stretch their money, and one of the areas they skimp on is child care. Often children are left alone at night or on weekends, which forces them to look after themselves and also provides ample time for mischief. Your preteen children need a responsible adult to provide security and direction.

In choosing a baby-sitter, try to find one who has a similar approach to child care as you. Then try to be consistent in the people you use.

If you can't afford such help, then you are going to have to come up with creative ways for providing it. Some single parents provide college students a spare room in exchange for baby-sitting after school and early evenings. Some have pooled their resources and hired joint baby-sitters or taken turns watching one another's kids. In one singles group, the younger singles without children provided a regular child care service to the single parents as their ministry to the group.

Whatever choice you make, it will require that you network with other needy parents.

——— **MAKE IT YOUR OWN** ———

❶ Which of the following is true of you?

- ☐ I never hire a baby-sitter.
- ☐ I never go out without my kids.
- ☐ I only allow family members to care for my kids.
- ☐ I have a good baby-sitter I regularly hire.
- ☐ My kids have a different baby-sitter every week.
- ☐ My kids go to a day care center each day I work.

❷ In what ways is your current child care arrangement a satisfactory one? _____

_____

_____

_____

❸ In what way is your current child care arrangement not satisfactory?

_____

_____

_____

4 What could you do to make the arrangement more satisfactory?

_____

_____

_____

Don't Allow Your Children to Become "Latchkey Kids"

Once again the issue becomes, "Can I afford day care?" I don't know if you can afford _not_ to provide it. Your preteen children need stable, adult supervision when they come home from school.

Check with your school district to see what other parents are doing. More and more local churches are providing some type of day care.

———— MAKE IT YOUR OWN ————

1 Which of the following apply to your situation?

☐ My kids go to a day care center after school.

☐ My kids go to the home of a friend or family member after school.

☐ My kids go home and fend for themselves.

2 What are your feelings about your current before and after school care? _____

_____

_____

_____

3 What are some alternatives? _____

_____

_____

4 Consider approaching your employer to see about a more flexible arrangement:

□ can you come in earlier and leave earlier?

□ could you work through your lunch hour and leave an hour early?

□ could you set up a room at your workplace where all the children of the single parents could play after school?

□ can you do some of your work at home?

HOW TO PICK A DAY-CARE CENTER

1. Ask about the ratio of children to day care workers. For infants and toddlers, one to four is good. Young children have an average need for one adult for every five or six children.

2. Ask about the training and credentials of the staff.

3. Observe the center in operation for a morning. Are the workers caring professionals? How do they comfort the children and how do they discipline?

4. Examine the facilities and equipment. Is the place clean and safe?

5. Find out what values they teach at the center. Are they Christian or even moral?

Adapted from *Christian Parenting and Child Care,*
by William Sears

Assign Chores in a Family Meeting

Most children complain that they have too many chores to do. Try to make the chores that have to be done around the house as fair and fun as possible. Do this in a family meeting where everybody can discuss the chores they don't mind and the ones they hate the most. Allow free discussion without judgment. Once everyone (including you) has spoken, let them know that everyone has to help, even though the tasks are not always enjoyable. You might start off by listing the tasks you are willing to do. Or you could even turn it into a game.

1 Which of the following is your experience?

☐ My kids do all their chores.

☐ We have clearly divided up the chores in our home.

☐ My kids have too many chores to do.

☐ My kids don't have enough chores to do.

☐ I have one child who willingly accepts major home responsibilities.

2 Which of my children feels overburdened? _____

3 Why might he or she feel this way? _____

_____

_____

_____

THE CHORES GAME

Write each chore on a 3 by 5 inch card. For each chore card, write a privilege card (a trip to the mall, lunch at McDonald's, a back rub, one hour of video games—whatever you or your children might enjoy).

Then deal all of the cards to all of the players. Each player gets one chore card for every privilege card. Be sure each family member gets an equal number of chores and privileges.

The players can now look at their "hands" and go around the circle trading chores and privileges. To make the game more interesting, add additional privileges so that you can "wheel and deal" more. For example, offering someone two hours of video games and a back rub in exchange for doing the laundry.

❹ How might I help? _____

_____

_____

Play this game weekly or monthly, so that you can rotate the chores, and build new opportunities for privileges. Do this as a family, and be sure that no one child gets overburdened with responsibilities.

Don't Give Your Children Adult Information

Some single-parent children grow up too fast because they are thrust into an adult world before they are ready. This includes giving them adult information that they don't need.

———— MAKE IT YOUR OWN ————

❶ Which of the following information have you shared with your children?

- ☐ Details about your dates
- ☐ Details about your ex-spouse's sexual exploits
- ☐ Information about financial problems
- ☐ Personal information about the divorce settlement and how far behind Dad is on his child support
- ☐ Physical affection between you and your dates
- ☐ Trips to the bedroom between you and your dates
- ☐ R-rated movies (and probably some PG's)
- ☐ All the things you hate about the other parent

This kind of information should not be discussed with your children. Don't mistake their maturity as an opening to vent all your feelings.

❷ In what ways do you rely on your children to provide

- ☐ emotional support _____

_____

☐ social support _____

_____

☐ financial support _____

_____

☐ physical support _____

_____

❸ How have you burdened your children? _____

_____

_____

_____

Sarah has lived alone with her mom for six years. There has been no contact with dad the entire time, which has merely driven mother and daughter closer together. They are each other's best friend. Mom shares just about everything with Sarah and vice versa. Unfortunately, mom has excluded all other relationships, leading to an unhealthy dependence on Sarah.

Now Sarah feels guilty for wanting to go away to college. Mom cries every time Sarah brings up the subject, so Sarah no longer mentions it. The pressure is mounting on Sarah to stay home for school even though she desperately wants to go to an out-of-town college.

Sarah's burden was in being her mother's best (and perhaps only) close friend, which meant she heard all about her mom's struggles and

> Children in single-parent families grow up fast, sometimes too fast. It is tempting for you to ease your own burdens by burdening them. Don't. Allow them to be children.

frustrations. What seemed like an enviable relationship to outsiders created an unhealthy bond that was destined to take its toll on both mother and daughter.

If you can identify some way that you have overly burdened your children, then you can also set the goal to try to improve this injustice. Write this goal here and in Appendix A. _____

_____

_____

_____

DISILLUSIONMENT AND DISTRESS

A third stressor on the children of single-parent families is the disillusionment and distress of having your family fall apart. Children begin to question the standards and belief system with which they grew up when their family falls apart.

As the parent, you probably are discredited as a role model and authority. They may still listen to you, but do you still represent the standards they want to live by when they grow up?

Many single-parent children no longer respect their parents' life-style or choices. Each event, each life stressor, adds to their sense of disillusionment and distress.

To help your child overcome these burdens, you will need to slowly rebuild their sense of trust and security in you.

After a period of time, most children return to a more balanced emotional state and mature spiritual state. Janet is a good example. Her father left the family for a younger woman with children of her own. He poured all of his attention into his newfound family and ignored her. From the time she was six until she was 21, Janet only saw her father a few times. Listen to her words describing her feelings about men.

> Since my dad was never around, I was uncomfortable around all men. I also grew to be angry at my mom because I blamed her for chasing my dad away. In my teenage years I gave her, and anyone else who tried to tell me what to do, a hard time. I rebelled against any authority figure. My pain became so intense that I ended up

talking to a counselor that I later learned was a youth minister. He listened to me and accepted me where I was. I don't remember him ever judging or condemning me. As I began to trust him, I realized that not *all* men were scum, and I began to gain a better understanding of my mom and what she had been through. You know I never really thought about how much pain she had endured, some caused by me, until I was almost 17.

Most importantly, my counselor taught me about the love of my heavenly Father. I have come to trust in Him as someone who will *never* leave me and whose love never varies. Through Him I can learn to love and trust others again. That doesn't mean that men don't still scare me sometimes, or that I don't experience insecurity from time to time, but now, I have the tools to work through it and can move forward, knowing that my Father is there to help me.

─────── MAKE IT YOUR OWN ───────

The graph traces major disillusionment, medium disillusionment, and mild disillusionment. Notice the trend toward renewed trust, over time. It is also possible that a person remains disillusioned

FIG. 6.1

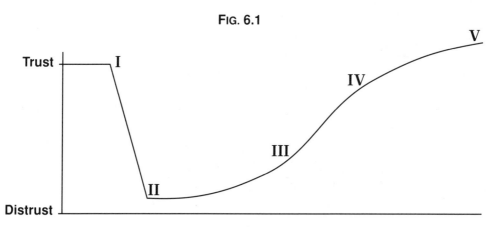

 I   Point of Family Breakup
 II Major Disillusionment
 III Medium Disillusionment
 IV Mild Disillusionment
 V   Renewed Trust

and distrustful through his or her life, and the rebuilding of trust is *not* a straight line as the graph might imply.

❶ Where would you put your child[ren] on the graph? Put an *X* on the place on the graph that best represents where they are depending on whether their disillusionment is mild, medium, or major. (Place a separate mark for each child.)

❷ What can you do to help edge your child[ren] toward renewed trust? Here are some suggestions but feel free to add your own.

- ☐ Give them space.
- ☐ Keep a positive spirit toward your situation and your ex.
- ☐ Explain to your kids exactly what happened.
- ☐ Be patient.
- ☐ Be honest about your own shortcomings but demand respect as a parent.
- ☐ Get involved in a church.
- ☐ Make sure your kids have other positive role models.

Action Point: Set a goal to work on at least one area that will help your children move from "disillusionment" toward "renewed trust." Write that goal here and in Appendix A.

7

Just for Dads

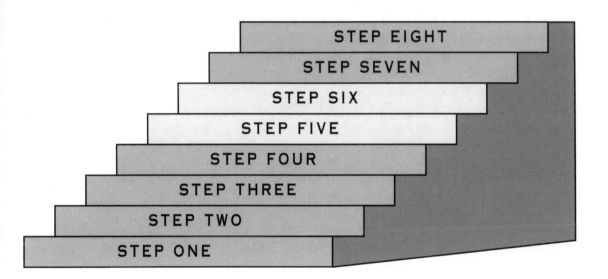

COROLLARY TO STEPS FIVE AND SIX

*If you are an absentee dad, determine to
maintain a healthy relationship
with your children.*

Even ten years later, I still vividly remember the most painful part of those early days following my divorce. It was when I came home at the end of a long day and put my key into the lock of my front door, knowing that there was nobody on the other side of the door. I deliberately avoided that moment by finding any excuse to not come home; running around in busy activities, trying to avoid the pain of my own loneliness.

I had not only lost the love of my wife, but I also lost my children. My wife had taken our three children and gone without leaving a note, phone number, or any indication of where she might be. It was months before I found out where she was and had a chance even to speak to my children by phone.

The loss and loneliness was so intense that it still brings tears to my eyes to talk about it. I can remember many, many months after my wife left, while I was cleaning my house, I was vacuuming under the sofa when I sucked up something that got caught in the nozzle. I reached in and pulled out a Lincoln Log. That's all it was—just a Lincoln Log—and yet, when I saw it, I began to sob. I cried long and hard. I had not truly grieved the loss of my children, and somehow this child's toy brought to the surface all of the pain and loss that I had been trying to avoid.

THE NEGATIVE MESSAGES

Most of this book has been directed to the custodial parents, usually moms. This chapter is just for dads, or the noncustodial parent.

Certainly there is much pain in losing your children. And every-other-weekend visits (if you're lucky) are hardly what you had in mind when you decided to start a family.

Only 40 percent of single dads see their children *at all* two years after the breakup. This statistic, while shocking, is easier to understand when you sit through men's support groups and listen to their stories of frustration, guilt, and confusion. Here are just some of the negative messages that we might hear or tell ourselves about our role as an absentee dad.

"It's Too Painful"

At a seminar recently, I listened as a tearful dad shared how he had lost contact with his children. They had moved about 600 miles away, and he was only able to see his children about once a month. The bigger problem was that—even after six months of divorce—he couldn't call his children without crying uncontrollably on the phone. Listen to how he describes it.

> I miss my children so much. Sometimes it's more than I can bear. When I look at their pictures, or hear their voices, I frequently burst into tears. I've tried calling or writing to them, but when I do, the result is the same. I become so emotionally distraught that I can't continue the conversation, or can't finish the letter. I don't want my children to see or hear me like this. I feel so weak and foolish.
>
> Now I must be emotionally blocked, because I try to stay busy in order to forget about them, and haven't written or called in months.

My advice to this man is to *let* your children see and hear you cry. It's better for them to see that you really *do* care for them, than to think you don't stay in touch because you don't love them.

————— **MAKE IT YOUR OWN** —————

❶ Is this your experience? If so, check the box below and beside it, write *when* you have felt this way most intensely.

☐ It's too painful._____

_____

❷ Now turn the negative statement into a positive one. It may be painful, but there are also joys involved in being with my kids. I especially enjoy it when _____

_____

"I No Longer Have Any Say"

Men tend to involve themselves in activities that they feel they can control or influence. Take away their influence or control, and they quickly lose interest. Psychologists say that this need for "significance" is one of a man's greatest emotional needs. For many, it's greater than their need for love.

My "significance" is my ability to influence my environment and to make a lasting impact on my world. That is why most men get their greatest satisfaction out of their work or their hobbies. Unfortunately, for many men work or a hobby is more satisfying than their marriages or their families. Some of you would probably admit that this was part of the reason for your marriage failure.

Ask men how they show love to their wives and children and they will respond with, "Look at all of the nice things I have provided! They live in a nice home, have good clothes, attend the best schools." In other words, "Look at how significant I am."

When a family experiences divorce, most of that significance is lost. The house is sold. The children go to public school, and the finances are a mess. Then your former wife gets a job, pays most of the bills herself, and makes all of the decisions about the kids without even consulting you. Within a few months or years, you've lost interest.

Here's how a couple of dads described their frustration:

> I did not approve of the way my former wife was raising the children, but every time I tried to discuss issues with her, it only led to more and more arguments. Unfortunately, she used these fights against me with the children; telling them how I refused to pay for their private schooling and their Nike sneakers. It made me look like the bad guy, when all I wanted was to be consulted before my wife made a major expenditure. But she just wanted me to send the money and keep my opinions to myself.

I know I shouldn't feel this way, but I now resent sending them anything. I think that's why I drag my feet when it comes to making those payments.

Another single dad described this scenario:

I know I should be more involved with my kids, but I'm just plain worn out. I've been banging my head against a wall for two years now. I feel like Sally [former wife] thwarts my efforts at every turn. She poisons me to the kids, and then comes up with every excuse for why they can't visit me on weekends. In the past six months I've only had three of my visiting weekends actually come about. They're either sick, too tired, too busy, or some other excuse.

When I'm actually with them, they gripe and whine about going home, and now all they talk about is how much fun they have with Steve, who I guess is mom's latest fling. I've come to the conclusion that everyone would be better off if I just faded out of the scene.

In both of these cases, these dads have lost their ability to have any say or influence in the lives of their children.

What can you do about it? You need to continue loving your children, no matter what! Your children need your involvement in their lives more than you realize. It is important to their psycho-sexual development, their interpersonal relationships, and their future marriage that you continue reaching out to them even if they emotionally slap your hands when you try to love them.

A recent caller told me, "My wife has moved away and refuses to let the children visit me. When I try to ask my children about it, they hang up on me. What should I do?"

My answer is the same. Don't give up. Continue to try to love them. I suggested that he write to his children regularly. Let them know that you still love them, miss them, and tell them what's going on in your life.

Your children will grow up some day. And when they do, they will begin to look at their family of origin in a more objective way. They will wonder what really happened between mom and dad. Then they will have an intense desire to get to know their real father. At that point, you want your children to think, "You know, my father always wrote to me or at least tried to reach out. No matter how we rejected him, he still loved us."

Just as adopted children go on a quest for their natural parents when they become young adults, so too will your children seek you out someday. When they do, what memories will they have of your efforts to love them?

———— MAKE IT YOUR OWN ————

❶ Is this your experience? If so, check the box below and beside it, write *when* you have felt this way most intensely.

☐ I no longer have any say._____

_____

Now turn the negative statement into a positive one.

❷ I don't have as much say as I used to, but I can still influence my kids' lives in these ways:_____

_____

_____

"I'm No Longer Needed"

When you feel that you have no say with your children, it affects your self-image as a father and eventually leads you to feel unneeded and even unwanted. But if your children are going to have any chance at overcoming the cycle of divorce and dysfunction in their lives, it is best accomplished by two parents committing themselves to coparenting in a healthy way. Assuming that you are a healthy influence on your children, you need to continue your efforts to have an effect on their lives.

Your children really do need a father figure. Research shows that without a father figure, girls may have a tendency toward sexual identity problems, may become promiscuous to gain attention from men, may marry someone who parents them, or may have difficulty in committed relationships.

Your sons, on the other hand, may experience a much lower self-image, may question their own masculinity, may have a greater likelihood of juvenile delinquency, or may fall into a cycle of chronic underachievement and underemployment.

───── MAKE IT YOUR OWN ─────

❶ Is this your experience? If so, check the box below and beside it, write *when* you have felt this way most intensely.

☐ I'm no longer needed._____

_____

Now turn the negative statement into a positive one.

❷ I *am* needed, maybe not in the same way I once was, but my kids still need me. This is what I can do for them:_____

_____

"I've Been Replaced"

Many men have the added pain of seeing their ex-wives take up with a new man. When kids are involved, it can hurt. You've been replaced! What could be harder than missing your children for weeks on end, finally getting them on the phone, and then spending the next half hour listening to how much fun they had on their camping trip with Mommy and that other man!

My friend Jeff knows what it's like to feel replaced even though he has primary custody of the kids. He can laugh now about something that happened to him once, but it hurt at the time. His wife had left him for another man, and occasionally the children would visit her and her boyfriend. Shortly after one of those visits, Jeff was talking with a friend who said, "I understand things are going pretty well with you and your wife. The Johnsons said they saw you together at the mall with the kids and you seemed to be getting along fine." Well, the Johnsons knew Jeff's wife but not Jeff, and they had actually seen her and the kids with her boyfriend. As Jeff puts it, "These people thought it was one big happy family, except he wasn't part of the family—yet."

While jealousy is a natural reaction, remember that there is no substitute for their real father. The distancing of their own flesh and blood is more devastating to children than the loss of any other relationship in their life.

Sean was a sixteen-year-old boy who was big for his age. He was referred to me for counseling while I was in the Philadelphia school district as a school psychologist. He had been a model student for the first eight years of his education, but in ninth grade his grades began to slip. He seemed to withdraw socially and eventually started getting into fights during recess and after school. He was sent to me so that I could find out if there was a reason.

In counseling, over a period of time, I heard about Sean's life with his mom and his mom's family, with whom he lived. His dad had left when he was just seven and moved about six blocks away. At first he saw his dad occasionally, but within a year his father stopped contacting him at all. He had a great relationship with his grandfather, who was retired and therefore became Sean's primary caretaker. Sean even called his grandfather "Papa."

I can only assume that Sean's father felt that he had been replaced. "They don't need me anymore," he must have reasoned. "He has Papa to take care of him."

So why was Sean having such problems? And why now, almost ten years after his dad's departure?

With tears in his eyes Sean asked me, "What is so wrong with me that my own father doesn't love me?"

"What makes you think he doesn't love you?" I asked.

Now sobbing so much that each sentence became labored, Sean responded, "He lives six blocks away, and I can count on one hand the number of times he has called to invite me over in the past five years. If I run into him in the street, he acts like a stranger. He seems so awkward, and then ends the conversation with 'we'll have to get together sometime.' I used to get my hopes up each time, but now I know he won't call. He was just saying that to be polite."

Sean's words demonstrate the fact that he needs his father. Even though he has a loving mother, a grandmother who is always there for him, and even a Papa who is probably his best friend; his dad has a special place in his heart. One that can't be replaced!

Why did it take so long for all of Sean's anger and insecurity to come to the surface? I can only conclude that he needed his dad all along, but the absence was merely "stuffed" at first. When he became a teenager, with all the changes he was going through, the unreturned love of his father was more than he could bear. He withdrew into a depression brought on by feelings of worthlessness, and eventually turned those feelings into anger, anger toward himself and aggressive anger toward whoever happened to be around. Counseling allowed him to express his anger in more appropriate ways.

——— **MAKE IT YOUR OWN** ———

❶ Is this your experience? If so, check the box below, and beside it write *when* you have felt that way most intensely.

☐ I've been replaced._____

_____

Now turn the negative statement into a positive one.

❷ My children may have a new stepfather, but he can never fully replace me as their real father. Here are the things that I can do for them that he can't:_____

_____

_____

"I'm a Failure as a Father"

Most of us feel like failures as fathers at some time or another. I've heard many humorous stories about dads who were trying to play "Mr. Mom," only to have everything fall apart. One dad told me of his experience as a fairly new single dad trying hard to impress his kids with how well he could do on his own. He made the dinner, cleaned the house, and separated the laundry into all of the proper piles. But when he started the washer, he forgot to put the drain into the sink. This allowed the soapy water to spill all over the floor.

Of course his two kids were the first to discover the mess, and they were afraid that Dad would be really mad when he saw what had happened. As he responded to their cries for help, he took one look at the floor and burst into laughter. They all three took a plunge into the mess and had a bubble bath in the middle of the kitchen.

One of my favorite stories was told by another dad who was trying to take good care of his children and was a little concerned about their coming home from school to an empty house. He was going to be at the office for a few hours while they were home alone after school, so he thought he should check in on them as soon as they were due home.

He called the house but got a strange man's voice on the other end of the line. He immediately hung up, assuming he had dialed the wrong number. He tried again and got the same strange voice. This time he asked the person, "Is this the _____ residence?"

The man stated, "You must have the wrong number."

This really perplexed him because he was sure he dialed the number correctly.

Just for safe measure, he painstakingly dialed his home number one more time and waited for the reply. Once again he got the same man's voice.

This time he hung up immediately and called the police, telling them that there was a strange man in his house and that his children were due home any minute. Would they please dispatch a car to his home as soon as possible?

As soon as he hung up, he jumped in his car and headed for home, making the usual half-hour ride in about twenty minutes.

As soon as he rounded the corner of his street, he could see the flashing lights of the police cars in front of his house. His children were standing in the front yard with a bewildered look on their faces.

"At least they're safe," he thought.

As he approached a police officer who seemed like he was in charge, the officer said, "Calm down. Everything will be fine. We searched the house and there's no one in there, but the house has been ransacked. Could you come in and take a look around and tell us what's missing."

As the gentleman entered his house, he quickly glanced over to see his TV, stereo, and VCR in their proper places. Then, when he realized what a mess the house was in, he turned to the officer and said, "But sir, this is the way I left it this morning."

The man's voice on the other end of the phone line turned out to be a repair person working on the phone lines at the end of the block.

While these stories are humorous, the fact that many of us feel like failures as fathers is not funny at all. The feelings of failure cause us to withdraw emotionally and maybe even assume that the kids would be better off without us. As stated before, this is certainly not the case.

———— MAKE IT YOUR OWN ————

❶ Is this your experience? If so, check the box below, and beside it write *when* you have felt that way most intensely.

☐ I'm a failure as a father._____

_____

Now turn the negative statement into a positive one.

❷ I may have made some serious mistakes as a father, but I'm not a total failure. With God's help, I will right some of these wrongs by

_____

_____

> You are needed in your children's lives. You may have made mistakes, and your present role in their lives may be diminished, but don't give up. They need you.

Action Point: Set a goal that you would like to accomplish with your children over the next several weeks. Write that goal here and in Appendix A._____

_____

_____

THE INFLUENCE OF A DAD

Decide for yourself. How great is a father's influence? How much of an influence was your father on you? Good or bad, much of what you are today is a reflection of your dad's values, or perhaps your attempt to measure up to your father's expectations. Some of us are still trying to prove things to our fathers.

If you came from a dysfunctional home, your father probably contributed to some unhealthy traits in your personality. You might even think that you would have been better off if your father had not been around at all. And you might suspect, in a moment of self-loathing, that your kids would be better off if you weren't around to pass on your own dysfunctional patterns.

But breaking the cycle for our children does not mean we walk away from our responsibilities—that will only perpetuate the dysfunction. It means that we recognize the dysfunctional pattern and determine that we will be different.

THE EXCEPTION TO THE RULE

I have given you the rule: Children of divorce do best when they maintain a consistent relationship with their father. To break the cycle of divorce and dysfunction with our children, we must stay actively involved in their lives. *However*, there is an exception. If you are very dysfunctional, such as emotionally, physically, or sexually abusive, it would be best for your children if you detached from them completely. My advice to these families is to get away from the abusing individual and begin to rebuild a new life for your children without the other parent. To the abusive parent, I would encourage you to detach from your family right now and work on your own issues until you are in a healthier emotional state. At that time you may be able to reconnect with your children. But even if you cannot, because of the extent of the hurt, at least you have not continued to perpetuate the abuse against your children.

A friend of mine recently shared a common example. He told me that his father never told him that he was proud of him or that he loved him. All his life this man, who is now an adult, tried to measure up to a standard he never understood, trying to please his father. His natural tendency would be to parent in the same rigid and unloving way. Instead, he determined that he would be different.

He told me that he made a vow that every time he sees his children he will tell them that he loves them, and then pick out something specific that he loves about them or that makes him proud. So far, he has kept that vow.

The task of being a father is not easy, and involves a variety of roles and responsibilities. Here are just a few.

Spiritual Leader

Trying to be spiritual head of your home becomes more and more difficult as you are separated from your children. In addition, we are battling the influences of an increasingly immoral society. It will require commitment, wisdom, and patience on your part (along with some divine intervention) for you to make a difference in the lives of your children.

When one thinks about a father's spiritual leadership, it is important to examine the father's commitment to God, as well as his ability to model those values to his children. A spiritual leader has the ability to turn daily events into teaching opportunities. This passive teaching technique is far more effective than forced Bible memorization or the empty repetition of prayers. These teaching opportunities arise whenever your children have questions about moral issues, interpersonal conflicts, minor stresses, and scholastic challenges.

Turn a resistance to church attendance into a discussion about the importance of worship. A discussion of the evening news is an opportunity to teach about God's worldview. Use a common frustration that your child shares with you as an opportunity to stop and pray for God's intervention. These lessons are most effective when they are natural and an outgrowth of your own life-style.

For women who are reading this, let me say that mothers can and should exercise spiritual leadership as well. If the father is not there or is not exercising a spiritual influence on the children, an extra responsibility falls on the mother.

The problem for noncustodial parents—whether fathers or mothers—is that you probably lack the structures you need to support your spiritual leadership. The sense of "home" is a bit strange when the kids are with you a few days each month. How can you build a habit of church attendance if you only see them every other Sunday? Daily prayers and Bible readings easily fall by the wayside if you're not with them day after day.

Let me suggest a biblical model for your spiritual life with your children. The ancient Israelites had the Temple, where the people prayed, sang, and gave sacrifices. But *before* the Temple was built, they had a tabernacle, which was basically a large tent. As the Israelites journeyed through the wilderness, they would stop and set up the tabernacle. Wherever they set it up became holy ground.

That's the way life is as a noncustodial parent. You have to set up your tabernacle wherever you can. Find those moments to sing and pray. Find those squares of holy ground where you can teach your kids to love God.

Another problem for all parents is that of responsibility and control. Spiritual leadership implies responsibility, but it does not mean that you are in control of your child's choices. Many parents suffer guilt when their children make wrong decisions. The son who is on drugs, the daughter who gets pregnant, or the child who rejects God—our response to them must still be one of love, but we must release our children to suffer the consequences of their own choices.

─────── **MAKE IT YOUR OWN** ───────

❶ In which of the following ways do you exercise spiritual leadership for your children?

☐ Read Bible with them.

☐ Pray before meals or at bedtime.

☐ Pray at other times with them.

☐ Take them to church.

☐ Talk about spiritual things with them.

☐ Be honest about your own spiritual needs.
☐ Pray for them.

❷ In what specific way can you exercise some spiritual leadership the next time you see or communicate with your kids?_____

_____

_____

Model Positive Masculinity

How do you define masculinity? In other words, what does it mean to be a man? It's not easy to explain, is it? It's even harder to *model* masculinity for your children.

In the broadest sense, I am merely referring to your need to be a positive male role model. All it means is that you can be yourself; share the things that you love with your children; and show them love, honesty, and commitment.

In *The Two Sides of Love*, John Trent and Gary Smalley discuss the "hard side" as well as the "soft side" of love. As men, we may tend to focus on the hard side of love, which means that we feel the need to be strong, tough, and to model tenacity to our children. While these skills are important, we must also model nurturing qualities, flexibility, affection, and self-sacrifice. Truly strong men balance both sides of this loving equation.

Balancing *both* sides of love is what comes to my mind when I think about being a positive male role model. We need to play ball, wrestle on the floor, and give "horsey" rides to our children, but we also need to cry; to express love and tenderness; and to listen to their ideas, interests, and concerns.

Our sons and daughters will have unrealistic and unbalanced expectations for men if they get the idea that masculinity only includes the hard side of love. We get enough of that from our male movie idols, such as John Wayne, Clint Eastwood, and Charles Bronson. While I love their movies, I resent what they taught me about what it meant to be a man. The types they play always have something big missing in their lives. They need no one, and they love no one. Can you imagine Clint Eastwood buying a self-help book such as this one? Or John Wayne going in for counseling? And if their "woman" leaves them, they just keep right on going. "No woman is worth crying over" is the message that comes through loud and clear. This is not what we want to model to our children.

Fathers send subtle and not-so-subtle messages to both their sons and daughters about how men walk, talk, dress, relate to one another, and relate to women. These lessons are important. Without them, our children would have a void in their lives. Statistics show that boys who are reared without a father

▶ have greater difficulty relating to other men

▶ don't know how to treat women

▶ have a higher rate of divorce

▶ don't know how to raise their own sons.

Daughters who are raised without a father figure

▶ have more difficulty relating to men

▶ may turn to sexuality as their only means of relating

▶ have a harder time choosing a husband

▶ and divorce those men at a higher rate than other women.

Obviously, it is important to *be there* for our kids. The danger with the hard side of love is that we can use it to avoid true intimacy with our children. We may be there physically for them but not there emotionally.

Many men play the "big boss" for their kids but never really develop relationships with them. In the name of discipline, we put up walls that keep us from being fully honest about ourselves. Discipline is an important expression of love—make no mistake. But if that's all there is, then the model we're showing our children is warped.

As men, we all have different interests, abilities, and personalities. Many of us work hard to develop certain skills or certain personality traits. But how hard have you worked on developing your ability to love your children? You may have the desire to love your kids, and that's a great start, but where does that desire take you? You may desire to be a great basketball player, but unless you hit the court day after day and practice your jump shot, it won't happen. Our desire to love needs to lead us into learning and practicing love for our kids.

And let's take that analogy further. A basketball player won't go very far if he has only a jump shot. He has to learn to drive with the ball, to rebound, to play defense. It's the same as we develop our ability to love our children. If we're only showing the hard side of love, we're one-dimensional dads. It won't be easy to learn those other loving skills—honesty, vulnerability, tenderness, compassion. It may take extra hours of practice.

MAKE IT YOUR OWN

❶ Which of the following do you consider most masculine? (Rank items within each group, with 1 being most masculine.)

Men

☐ Sylvester Stallone ☐ Alan Alda ☐ Bill Cosby
☐ Phil Donahue ☐ Ronald Reagan ☐ Jimmy Carter
☐ Tom Brokaw ☐ Peter Jennings ☐ Dan Rather

Games

☐ Baseball ☐ Ice Hockey ☐ Tennis
☐ Football ☐ Golf ☐ Chess

TV Shows

☐ "Jeopardy" ☐ "Wheel of Fortune" ☐ "The A-Team"
☐ "60 Minutes" ☐ "Dynasty" ☐ "Quantum Leap"

Activities

☐ Making lots of money ☐ Volunteering to tutor inner-city kids
☐ Picking up the check ☐ Donating money to an inner-city tutoring center
☐ Discussing politics ☐ Snoring

Magazines

- ☐ *Newsweek*
- ☐ *Playboy*
- ☐ *Sports Illustrated*
- ☐ *Road and Track*
- ☐ *Popular Mechanics*
- ☐ *Consumer Reports*

Vehicles

- ☐ Jeep
- ☐ VW Beetle
- ☐ Corvette
- ☐ Pickup truck
- ☐ Camaro
- ☐ Station wagon

❷ Now look over your choices. *Why* did you rank them as you did? Giving it some more thought, do you want to change any of the rankings?_____

❸ Of the following qualities, what image of masculinity do you want your children to have? (Rank items from 1 to 12, with 1 being quality you most want children to have.)

- ☐ caring
- ☐ giving
- ☐ athletic
- ☐ tough
- ☐ capable
- ☐ suave
- ☐ strong
- ☐ honest
- ☐ loyal
- ☐ tender
- ☐ self-confident
- ☐ emotional

❹ How can you best model masculinity for your kids? (Rank items from 1 to 9, with 1 being the best.)

- ☐ Practicing severe discipline
- ☐ Being open about your own needs
- ☐ Maintaining a strong "in control" image
- ☐ Being concerned about the details of their lives
- ☐ Giving them the money and objects they need
- ☐ Showing emotion
- ☐ Succeeding at everything you attempt
- ☐ Focusing on the things you do well
- ☐ Demanding perfection (or near-perfection) from your kids

Naturally, each man is different. The point is this: Don't be swayed by our culture's stereotypes. Be the "total man" you are, with your emotions and doubts, as well as your strength and courage. Allow your children to see the real you, not some phony "masculine" facade.

Many marriages have crumbled because the partners didn't allow themselves (or their spouses) to be themselves. They demanded certain images of masculinity and femininity that really had no basis in reality. You can help break the cycle in your kids by putting aside those false images and being the full man you are.

Spend Time with Each Child

Previously, while addressing the custodial parent, I talked about the need to spend individual time with each child. The same principle is true for the noncustodial parent. Even though you usually get the children all together on an occasional basis, it is important that you spend individual time with each child. One on one, you gain insights into their hopes, dreams, trials, and insecurities. Bonding in this way will have a lasting impact on you and your children.

During these individual times, try to focus on how your children feel about themselves, how they are doing in school, where their peer relationships are going, and how they are doing spiritually. Glean this information from your natural conversations about their lives and how they are doing.

This is also an excellent time for you to convey to your children how much you love them, what you specifically love about them, how you want to be involved in their lives, and perhaps even some of your own struggles. Guard against any inclination to use this as a preaching opportunity. Preaching will take away quickly the specialness of the occasion.

You can accomplish these one-on-one visits by alternating special trips or camping trips with each child, or by spending one weekday evening or morning with a different child. All of this, however, requires their mother's cooperation. I hope for the sake of your children, you will cooperate toward helping *each other* spend individual time with each of your children.

——— MAKE IT YOUR OWN ———

(If you have only one child, you may skip this section.)

❶ When was the last time you spent individual time with each of your children? What did you do? For how long a period? What did you learn about your children, and what did your children learn about you?

❷ Child's name _____

When? What? How long?_____

_____

_____

What did you learn about him/her?_____

_____

_____

What did he/she learn about you?_____

_____

_____

❸ Child's name _____

When? What? How long?_____

_____

_____

What did you learn about him/her?_____

_____

_____

What did he/she learn about you?_____

_____

_____

❹ Child's name_____

When? What? How long?_____

_____

_____

What did you learn about him/her?_____

_____

_____

What did he/she learn about you?_____

_____

_____

[Repeat on a separate sheet for other children.]

Build Special Times and Memories

While I do not advocate the temptation to become a "Disneyland Dad," it is important that you build memories and special times with your children. These memories can be almost anything from pictures of a camping or fishing trip, to a special breakfast place that you frequent. These special times become part of the bonding process. Every experience you have with your child—even when it's not necessarily positive—creates a bond between you and your children.

"Remember the time we went camping and it rained the whole time? What a mess, but it was so funny when we finally gave up and went to McDonald's for lunch. That was the best food we ever tasted."

"Remember how we used to go to that same breakfast place every Saturday, that is, until you found that fly in your food? That was so funny."

"I'll never forget when you got sick in the middle of the church service and had to run out down the center aisle of the church."

Our children will remember the strangest things. Keeping a scrapbook or photo album of "Things I did with my Dad" might be a fun project for everyone. If you have trouble coming up with ideas, just ask your children what they like to do. Model rocketry, collecting stamps, a drive in the country, or a visit to the barber shop together might be activities that will make a lasting impact on both you and your children.

———— **MAKE IT YOUR OWN** ————

1 You may want to ask your kids for help with this one. What do they remember about times you've had together?

Special places_____

_____

Special events_____

_____

Funny experiences_____

_____

Other stuff_____

_____

2 What other special moments could you plan to share with your kids in the next year?

_____

_____

_____

_____

Build Responsibility and Independence

The final task that we will mention in this section is one that often gets lost in the need to have fun every weekend. But is essential if we are to be the positive male role model that we want to become.

We need to build a sense of responsibility and independence in our children. We must first model these traits and then teach our children through discussion.

Your task is not to develop clones of yourself, but to help your children to become self-sufficient men and women who follow God's calling, independent of *your* goals for their lives. Any attempt to thwart this move toward independence will stifle their natural development and probably result in their resentment of your efforts to control or manipulate.

One boy recently told me of his dad's passion for football. "My dad played in high school and college, and I guess he always expected that I'd do the same. When I joined the school play in high school, at the expense of the football team, he was livid. Of course he blamed my mom for making me a sissy and undermining his authority. The whole issue became a sore subject for many years. My dad and I still can't watch a football game together without his making some wise crack about my 'acting career,' or starting some kind of fight."

Teaching responsibility is an important job for both parents and must begin by example. Do you keep your word to your children and to others? When you say you will be somewhere at a certain time, do you follow through? And when you've made a commitment, what do you do when a much better offer comes along?

"Son, I know we said we'd help out at the church clean-up day on Saturday, but guess what—I got free tickets to the big game, and they're on the 50-yard line."

This example presents an ideal learning opportunity for you and your child. You may consider several responsible options and several irresponsible ones. Discuss these issues in a way that will teach your child responsibility.

"Son, we made a previous commitment to help out at the church, and as much as I'd like to go to the game, we need to keep that commitment."

Or, "Perhaps we could see if we could get someone to take our place at the church this week, and then do double duty next time."

Or, "Let's call the church and see if there would be a way for us to keep our commitment to them and still make the game."

If we shrug off responsibility as if it's really not that important, then we send a message to our child about handling responsibility.

❶ On a scale of 1 to 10 (10 is most), how independent are your children?

Child:_____ _____

Child:_____ _____

Child:_____ _____

❷ On the same scale, how much do you promote your children's independence?_____

What could you do to promote more independence in your children:

_____

_____

❸ On a scale of 1 to 10, how responsible are your children?

Child:_____ _____

Child:_____ _____

Child:_____ _____

❹ On the same scale, how responsible are you?_____

❺ What can you do to promote more responsibility in your children?

_____

_____

You are a major source of your children's self-image and their primary model of masculinity. As you transmit values to them and build a unique relationship in the short time available, you can help them grow into responsible adults.

MAINTAINING A LONG-DISTANCE RELATIONSHIP

One of the hardest parts of being a single dad is when distance or circumstances separate you from your children. Many dads either don't see their children at all or see them for only a few weeks of the year. Their question to me is usually twofold: How can I have a relationship with my child? And can I really make any kind of impact in my child's life?

The answer to the second question is a hearty Yes! You can still have a profound impact on your children. The other question is much harder to answer. How in the world can I have a relationship that really affects my children?

Below are some general guidelines for developing a long-distance relationship. Use your own creativity and determination to apply the principles to your own situation.

Guideline 1: Stay in Touch with Your Children

Many dads allow frustration and rejection to kill their determination to maintain contact. As hard as it may be at times, stay in touch with your children! If your children won't accept your calls, send them cards and letters. If they send the letters back, keep them for the future but continue sending cards and notes, at least on all special occasions.

Some day your children will be curious about their dad. Some day they are going to want to find out for themselves what you are like. And when that day comes, you will have a collection of letters that you sent them. What a great way to review the years and to prove to them in a concrete way that you never stopped loving them or thinking about them.

On a radio talk show, a man called me and tearfully described his loss of contact with his children due to a court order. His wife had accused him of sexually abusing his children and the court forbade him to visit or even call. He claimed that he had done nothing, but he had given up on ever talking to his children again. His question to me was, "What can I do to let my children know that I still love them and think about them?"

I had no way of knowing whether or not he had done anything wrong, but I knew that either way, he should at least be able to write to his children and tell them how he felt about them. I encouraged him first and foremost to obey whatever court order he was under. However, if it was permissible, I urged him to send his children a brief note or card. I specifically told him to avoid any reference to the legal problems, but merely tell them of his love. Then, depending on their reaction, he might consider regular notes. I believe that in spite of everything, his children will someday wonder about him and may want to contact him. It would be better for them if they knew how to reach him and if they knew of his feelings toward them.

For most of us, our contacts are not so restricted, and therefore it is critical that we keep in touch through phone calls, cards, notes, and letters.

——————— **MAKE IT YOUR OWN** ———————

❶ How many times in the last month have you contacted your children?_____

❷ Should you contact them more often?_____

❸ What could you do to improve this frequency of contact?_____

Guideline 2: Make It Easy for Your Children to Contact You

Maintaining a long-distance relationship also requires that your children have easy access to you—wherever possible, at any time or place. If you are a business person, get a private work number or maybe even a private "beeper" for your children. Some dads have gotten an 800 number so their children can call them wherever they are, without worrying about charges. If not that, at least give your children permission to call collect at any time. The goal is to remove all obstacles and difficulties that might inhibit their calling or writing.

Other methods might include giving your children a computer with a modem or sending audio or video tapes back and forth. The least expensive way is to correspond through the mail, in which case it would help to send them self-addressed, stamped envelopes, or prepaid postcards. One desperate father showed me a card designed for his children, which was prewritten in the following form.

Dear Dad,

We are doing   ☐ great

                  ☐ fine

                  ☐ okay

                  ☐ not so good

In school, things are . . .

_____

_____

The entire note was a series of multiple choice items that only required their checking the appropriate box. It was meant to be humorous, but it was effective in getting his children to respond.

I have a friend who has three children on the East Coast while he lives in California. It really hurts him that he has to be separated from his children, but his work forces him to be so far away. He would never claim to be a super dad, but he does a conscientious job at maintaining a great relationship with his children. He uses his frequent flier mileage to fly his children in for several weeks a year. He also makes sure that he sees each of them for a one-on-one visit at least every year. He also carries a beeper with him at all times so that his children can reach him at any time no matter where he goes.

I was with his son one time when we were discussing an important issue, which we couldn't resolve. The youth interjected, "Let's ask my dad what he thinks."

I shot back, "Oh sure, he's in California. By the time you ask him it will be too late to do any good."

To my surprise his son replied, "What do you mean? We can ask him right now. Just dial this 1-800 number and then type in your number here, and my dad will call us within a minute or two."

Oh, the wonders of modern technology. Sure enough, his dad called right away. He resolved the issue for us, but even more impressively, I learned that he was in the middle of a shopping center and had called us from a pay phone. There was never a hint of annoyance in his voice. I don't know very many children who have better access to their fathers than this child, even among those who live with their dads.

──────── **MAKE IT YOUR OWN** ────────

❶ On a scale of 1 to 10, how easy is it for your kids to contact you (10 is easiest)?_____

❷ What one thing can you do to make this contact easier?_____

Guideline 3: Find Some Common Interests

Even though you are separated by miles, a common interest can bring you together. Here are a few examples of this guideline:

▶ Play chess or some other game by sending your moves to each other through the mail.

▶ Follow a sports team together, and then agree to watch the event together in your separate locations. Set a time to discuss the game—at halftime or soon after the conclusion.

▶ Watch or rent the same movies and then critique them by phone or mail.

▶ Collect stamps, coins, cards, or whatever, and then trade with each other through the mail.

▶ Swap items that your city is famous for.

▶ Keep a notepad on the refrigerator, by the phone, or in your briefcase, and jot down things that you want to talk with your kids about. Encourage your kids to do the same. Refer to this list when you do talk with your kids.

▶ Keep a file of interesting newspaper or magazine clippings, or inter-

TEN COMMANDMENTS FOR DADS

1. Thou shalt love your children and demonstrate that love in concrete and specific ways.

2. Thou shalt not lose contact with your children despite any length of time or distance.

3. Thou shalt not speak ill of your children's mother but refer to her with respect and loving honesty.

4. Thou shalt resist the urge to be a "Disneyland Dad" but instead seek a quality relationship with your children.

5. Thou shalt spend individual time with each of your children.

6. Thou shalt not put your children in the middle by making them choose between you and their mother.

7. Thou shalt not use your children as spies or messengers between you and their mother.

8. Thou shalt seek to find some common areas of interest to share with your children.

9. Thou shalt make it easy for your children to stay in touch with you when they are not with you.

10. Thou shalt do your best to cooperate with the other parent toward a coparenting relationship.

esting photos, that you run across that would interest your kids. Send these every month of so.

▶ Subscribe to a youth-oriented magazine and send a gift-subscription to your child. Talk about the articles in it.

▶ Watch a TV show together. Plan that both you and your child will watch a "family special" and then talk about it. You could even call each other during commercial breaks or (if the charges aren't prohibitive) stay on the line during the show.

▶ Start a joke-of-the-week pattern. If you call your child on a weekly basis, challenge him or her (and yourself) to come up with a new joke to tell each week.

▶ Help with homework. Offer to help your child by phone or mail with homework or school projects. Maybe you could gather some information and send it along.

▶ Give a specialized calendar. This will take some preparation, but it would make a great Christmas gift. Get one of those page-a-day calendars and write a message for each day. Write funny things, loving things, spiritual things, wise things—whatever comes to mind. Then, each day of the next year, your child will be getting a message from you.

Action Point: What specific changes will you make in your contact with your children in the next few weeks in order to build a better relationship? Write it here in the form of a goal and again in Appendix A.

_____

_____

_____

From Dating to Remarriage

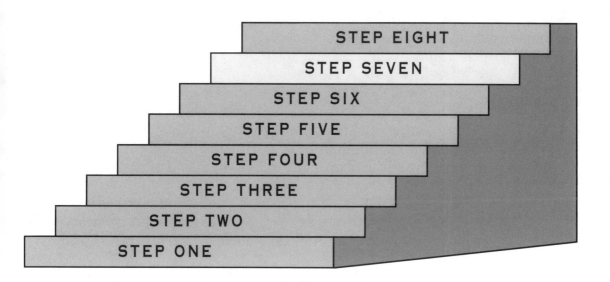

STEP EIGHT

STEP SEVEN

STEP SIX

STEP FIVE

STEP FOUR

STEP THREE

STEP TWO

STEP ONE

STEP SEVEN

Determine to make your social life healthy for you and your children.

Time has gone by. You're recovering nicely. You begin noticing the other sex again. And then there's a special someone you decide you want to date. But how? Where do you start? How do you let the other person know you're interested? How do you shield yourself from the pain of rejection? How do you ask a person out? How do you dial the phone?

You feel like you're fifteen again, fumbling around, swooning, practicing your lines, preening in front of the mirror. You feel all of the confusion, embarrassment, and discomfort of a high-school freshman. And then your kid says, "Cool it. It's no big deal."

Dating is hard enough. Dating the second time around is harder. Having children complicates things even more. And it cuts both ways: children complicate your dating life, and dating complicates your childrearing.

Many of us have used our children as an excuse to avoid the morass of a dating life. Who has time for dates? Will my dates disrupt my children? Will the fact that I have kids be a turnoff? But sooner or later, most of us plunge back in. When we do, there's a ton of things to deal with, for us and our children.

You may have never been married, or be widowed or divorced, but one thing we all have in common is the brokenness of a lost relationship. After any such breakup, there is a normal period of grieving. People need to work through this grief—through all those stages we talked about earlier—before they enter a healthy new romance. Many people rush into new relationships, assuming that a new romance will heal the hurts of the old one. That seldom works. As a single parent, you are making choices that affect your whole family; your kids are just as vulnerable at this stage as you are.

Take the time to heal properly. And even then, be careful as you re-enter the dating scene. If you are to break the cycle of divorce and dysfunction, then you need to take a serious look at the type of decision-making that goes into your dating.

You will need to evaluate the factors that led to the breakup of your previous relationship. What choices proved to be unwise? On what values did you base those choices? Do you need to reconsider those values? What aspects of your personality need work? You need to evaluate honestly your problem areas. Be aware of these as you begin to develop new relationships.

Forgiveness is also crucial. You have to come to a place of peace in your attitudes toward your ex. If you don't, many problems await you in future relationships.

You may end up in a "revenge relationship," where the whole point is to get back at the person who hurt you. Your values then get distorted. You're no longer looking for the person who's right for *you*, but for the one who will score the most jealousy points with your ex.

Or you may find yourself fighting all the old battles in your new relationship. Or you find it impossible to trust anyone. Dating becomes a game that you try to win. But you shield yourself from intimacy. Such shielding is a natural defense mechanism. In the first few years after a divorce, it is perfectly normal to hold back. But some people never allow themselves to trust another. They date but refuse to commit. Some even remarry but refuse to invest themselves fully in the marriage. And it all goes back to forgiveness. The offense of that first breakup was never resolved.

> Before you begin to date in earnest, make sure you have completed the grieving process and are emotionally healthy enough to begin anew.

COMMON DIFFICULTIES

As we begin to think about dating, we first must deal with some issues that commonly confront the single parent who is trying to re-enter the single life-style.

Who Am I Anyway?

Any breakup affects your *identity*. (This includes the death of a spouse.) In any marriage, identities merge to some degree. Married people do not lose their individuality, but as the Bible says, "The two become one." They share living quarters, finances, children, dreams, goals, and even names.

What happens when "the one becomes two"? You have to carve a new space for yourself, a new personhood. This can be difficult. Many divorced couples have experienced the tedious process of sorting through their belongings. Who gets the house? Who gets the kids? Who gets the church? Who gets the friends? Who gets the photo album and the memories that go with it?

It is never easy to unravel the strands of a life that has been knotted to another. Who are you—by yourself, on your own, without that other person?

Well, you're a parent, for one thing. For many newly single people with kids, that's the one shred of self-image they have left. I'm a mommy; I'm a daddy. I will do my best to care for these kids of mine. We are still a family.

And then the day comes when you realize that you're more than a parent. You are a single man or woman with a certain amount of desire and appeal for the opposite sex. It can be an exciting and fearful moment. You suddenly have a new identity. You are a sexual being again. Romance has returned.

But there are some dangers here. Plunging into a new romantic relationship can *keep* you from establishing your own identity. Sure, it may awaken a whole new side of your personality, but make sure you coordinate that side with the rest of you.

So who are you? Ask yourself this crucial question *before* you get involved in a new relationship. Take an inventory of your talents, desires, and personality traits.

Then begin to *develop* your identity. Discover some new talents. Fulfill some wholesome desires. Your role as a parent will always be a part of your identity, but what kind of a parent are you? How do you see your personality rubbing off on your kids?

But don't limit your world to your children exclusively. Expand your horizons; meet new people. Look for people you want to be like, and hang around with them.

What does all this have to do with dating and romance? Simply this: If you have not come to terms with your own identity, you will have little to offer in a new relationship. What's worse, you could find your identity affected in unhealthy ways in a bad relationship. You could become a chameleon whose values are determined by anyone who shows an interest. If your values, life-style, and self-image are well-grounded beforehand, then you can start a new relationship on a solid foundation.

A woman recently told me of her own disastrous dating experience. She told me that she had been married twice, the second being a rebound relationship that should have never happened. Now being single yet again, she said she didn't want to make another mistake. She was trying to be cautious about those she dated. Her problem, however, was that men frequently pressured her to sleep with them after the first few dates.

"Well!" she proclaimed. "I don't care *how* good-looking they are, I'm not that kind of person."

Her question to me was, "How can I continue dating when all men expect me to sleep with them by the third date?"

She asked me this question at a Fresh Start seminar in a church with about a hundred and fifty other people present. I asked the audience, "Are all men like that?" There was a resounding NO from the crowd. (And then a few muffled yesses, accompanied by some lingering snickers.)

Yes, I told the group, there are plenty of men out there who *are* like that, but there are places to go where you can meet different kinds of people. If you have set certain standards for your life, then your only chance of keeping to those standards is to date people with the same convictions. I told this woman that the church singles' group would be a better place to find dates than the local singles' bar.

Fortunately, she had been able to determine that a crucial part of her own identity was sexual responsibility. If she had not previously determined that, she might easily have been swayed by any of the men she dated, with disastrous consequences for her own emotional health.

——— MAKE IT YOUR OWN ———

❶ How would you describe yourself? (check all that apply)

☐ Happy	☐ Thoughtful	☐ Energetic	☐ Caring
☐ Laid-back	☐ Moral	☐ Adventurous	☐ Timid
☐ Religious	☐ Honest	☐ Loyal	☐ Musical
☐ Fun-loving	☐ Eager to please	☐ Artistic	☐ Creative
☐ A good parent	☐ Perfectionist	☐ A bit odd	☐ Athletic

❷ What three other adjectives describe you?_____

_____

_____

_____

❸ What quality do you wish you had more of?_____

_____

❹ What is one of your positive qualities that you see having an impact on your child[ren]?_____

❺ How do you see this? (Give an example.)_____

_____

_____

_____

❻ Which of the following activities would you find interesting? (If you are already involved in one of these activities, put an X in the space; if you're not, but think it would be good for you, put an O.)

- [ ] Community or church choir
- [ ] Community or school theater group
- [ ] Art or dance classes
- [ ] Night school for professional advancement
- [ ] Night school for general interest
- [ ] Bowling league
- [ ] Health club
- [ ] Volleyball or other athletic group
- [ ] Home Bible study
- [ ] Church singles' group
- [ ] Community singles' group
- [ ] Divorced/widowed support group
- [ ] Parent-Teacher Association (PTA)
- [ ] Volunteer work for a community charity
- [ ] Environmental group

Now look at the list of qualities you felt described yourself. Which of the activities just listed seems to fit your qualities the best. (Put a *Q* next to that activity.) Consider the quality you said you wanted more of. Which of the activities listed seems to fit that desired quality the best? (Put a *W* for Want next to that activity.)

Now interpret your activity list:

If you have a lot of X's, you're already doing a lot. You probably can't add much more. If your *X's* include your *Q* activity and your *W* activity, great! If not, you may need to ease out of something you're doing now, in order to become involved in things that will help support who you are and who you want to be.

If you have a lot of O's, you'll have to choose. You can't do it all. Look at your *W* activity. Is that something you can do right away, or does it scare you? If you can do it, make that a priority. If not, choose your *Q* activity, or one of your *O's* to get "warmed up." But don't put off your *W* activity indefinitely. That's where you want to go.

If you haven't checked much of anything, wake up! You still may be cocooning with your kids. This is natural in the period immediately following a divorce or the death of a spouse. You may not have much desire for social activities—*and that's fine*. Don't rush it. If it's been a year-and-a-half or two years since the divorce or death, push yourself a little. Choose your Q activity, or another activity from the list that's nonthreatening. It may be time to spread your wings socially. But be wary of romantic involvement at this stage. You need to feel comfortable with people in general before you take up with one special person again.

Action Point: If you have decided to pursue a social activity, find out whom you need to contact to get involved. Write that person's name and number or address here, along with the date you will make that contact. Write that activity on your list of goals in Appendix A.

Name_____

Number or Address_____

_____

Date to Contact:_____

Who'd Want Me?

Self-doubt and insecurity also plague single parents. Part of this is the aftermath of the broken relationship that led to our singleness; some may be baggage from our childhood. And then there's always the question "Who would want someone with two young children and a bunch of bills?"

These feelings of inferiority may be unhealthy, but they are certainly understandable. After all, we've just been rejected by the ones who supposedly knew us best. So we tend to think that we must not be worth very much.

I've been there. While I didn't have children to deal with, my divorce was devastating to my self-image. I felt like a complete failure. If I couldn't keep my marriage together, then what could I do? I felt good for nothing.

This feeling persisted for years after the divorce. Many of the other aspects of recovery had kicked in. I had stepped back into the world. I was working on my graduate degree in counseling—and *still* these self-doubts were afflicting me. Every book I studied seemed to taunt me: "If you couldn't make your own marriage work, how can you help anyone else?" Yes, I was stepping forward in my career, but those nagging doubts were always a step behind me.

Everywhere I went, I took those doubts with me. I'd enter a room and think, "These people don't care about me. They see right through me. They know how stupid I really am." Have you felt that way, too? It becomes a kind of walking paranoia. We twist every compliment into an insult and every insult—even if offered in fun—cuts deep.

The same principle applies as in the identity crisis. If you don't know who you are, you're in no position to match up with a new mate. And if you think you know who you are, and you think you're awful, you're in an even worse position. A poor self-image will lead to poor choices in relationships—especially marriage relationships. You don't need this. Your kids don't need this. We want to break the cycle of divorce. That has to start with the rebuilding of the individuals in the family. It has to start with you.

How often have you seen low self-esteem lead to twisted relationships? The self-doubter runs away from a "good" partner, fearing that the partner is "too good for me." Often the self-doubter ends up with an abusive partner, one who confirms all those doubts the person started with: "I'm no good. I don't deserve any better." Obviously, if children are involved, they bear the brunt of this abuse as well. They grow up feeling unworthy of real love, and they make bad decisions in adulthood. The cycle continues.

Chances are, your self-image is low right now. Chances are, you are vulnerable. You are susceptible to rebound relationships. You are susceptible to unhealthy choices. You are a bundle of needs, and if the right person of the opposite sex comes along whispering sweet nothings and promising the moon, you're gone.

> Your self-image affects the type of relationships in which you get involved. A poor self-image can lead to unhealthy dating relationships.

How can you protect yourself? Take the time to bolster your self-image. Find friends (not lovers) who will encourage you. Practice uplifting self-talk. Challenge your self-critical statements and replace them with self-affirmation. Examine your various needs and try to meet them in nonsexual ways.

———— MAKE IT YOUR OWN ————

Take the following test of your self-image to see how much work you still need to do.

❶ When you get up in the morning and look at yourself in the mirror, which thoughts are most likely to enter your mind?

☐ "God sure did make me cute."

☐ "Oh well, I'll make the most of what I've got."

☐ "What a mess."

❷ When you walk into a room of people you don't know, which are you most likely to think?

☐ "I wonder how many interesting people I can meet."

☐ "I wonder where the food is."

☐ "These people don't want to talk to me."

❸ When faced with a new challenge, which is most likely to enter your mind?

☐ "I'm looking forward to this."

☐ "I wonder how I'll do."

☐ "I'll probably mess things up."

❹ When asked to address a small group, which would you feel?

☐ intrigued

☐ a little nervous

☐ petrified

❺ While waiting for your blind date to arrive, which are you most likely to think?

- ☐ "I wonder what he/she will look like."
- ☐ "I wonder what he/she will think of me."
- ☐ "I know he/she will be disappointed in me."

❻ When going to a parent/teacher conference, which are you most likely to think?

- ☐ "I wonder how this will help my children in school."
- ☐ "I wonder if I'm doing something wrong."
- ☐ "I hope the teacher doesn't know what a bad parent I am."

❼ When in a conversation with a relatively new acquaintance, which are you most likely to think?

- ☐ "I have a good point I think I can add here."
- ☐ "I wonder what I can say?"
- ☐ "Anything I add will probably sound stupid."

❽ On a typical work day, which thought do you think most often?

- ☐ "They're getting more than their money's worth out of me."
- ☐ "I'm doing the best I can."
- ☐ "I hope they don't figure out how incompetent I am."

❾ When unexpected guests drop by, what's your overriding feeling?

- ☐ "How nice, a friendly visit."
- ☐ "I hope I put the dirty laundry away."
- ☐ "They'll see what a terrible housekeeper I am."

❿ If I asked you to write three things that you liked about yourself and three things you didn't like about yourself, which of the following statements would be true?

- ☐ "I could come up with three likes and three dislikes pretty easily."
- ☐ "I would have to think for a while about both likes and dislikes."

☐ "I could give you the dislikes pretty quickly, but I would have to think pretty hard to come up with any likes."

Now look back over your test. The first choice for each question is a fairly healthy response. The second choice is neutral, while the third choice indicates a negative self-image.

If your responses were mostly from the first choice category, then you have a fairly healthy self-image. Neutral responses are okay. They probably indicate that you have some insecurities.

If your responses fell mostly in the third choice category, then your self-image is fairly negative, and you probably need to do some work on developing a more positive self-image before you attempt a serious relationship. Also bear in mind that your children will reflect your self-image. You may be passing this unhealthy cycle onto your children. I would recommend counseling, or at least a book on developing a better self-image. See Appendix B.

Action Point: If you scored low on the self-image test, you need to begin work on it as soon as possible. Set a goal to get a book on the topic or to begin counseling that will focus on building your self-image. Write that goal here with a time frame in which to do it, and record it again in Appendix A.

_____

_____

_____

The Need Trap

A bundle of needs—that's what I called you—especially with kids, especially without a spouse. You probably need money, time, rest, intelligent conversation, and a big hug. You can pretend to be self-sufficient, but those needs keep creeping up.

A new romantic relationship may promise to meet those needs. However, a relationship built on need-meeting is, by definition, *codependent*. That doesn't mean that husbands and wives can't meet each other's needs, but if you enter a relationship in an extremely empty or needy state, the relationship will lack wholeness. It will always have an off-center quality.

Healthy relationships are give *and* take. *Both* partners fill the gaps in the other's life. You and your children need to take time to heal. The departure of your spouse left a hole in your life. Let the hole heal up. Let the "hole" become "whole," before you seek new intimacies.

About three years after my divorce, I started dating a woman I met in the singles' group at church. She was a very giving person, always wanting to tend to my needs. Naturally, I was attracted to that. I had a lot of needs.

We hit it off right away, seeing each other almost every day. After three months or so, she started to ask me where the relationship was going. I was the typical noncommittal male; I was happy to have her cook for me, but I didn't want to get serious.

Six months into the relationship, eight months, the question kept coming: "You know, Tom, I just need to get some idea of where this relationship is going." And I would regularly shrug it off.

As I think back on it, I feel like a real creep. But I wasn't trying to take advantage of her. I just wasn't ready for a committed relationship. Our romance had grown too quickly. She was ready for commitment, but I still had some healing to do.

You could probably guess the end of this story. A few months later, we broke up. It was painful for both of us, but there was no way to stay together. She was wasting her time with me.

You may be in some rebound relationship based on need, but your heart hasn't healed. This relationship can't provide the healing you need.

So then, how do you deal with the many needs you're suddenly experiencing? Lean on your friends for emotional support, companionship, and intellectual stimulation. If you don't have a network of friends reaching out to you, reach out to them!

Meeting people may be the last thing you want to do right now. You probably are experiencing a tension between the need for love and the need for protection. You want to reach out, but you're afraid because your emotions are so vulnerable. Accept those feelings and go slow—even with friendships. Reach out in low-risk ways to people you can count on. Learn what people you can trust and then trust them. Don't stop with one person, but keep reaching out until you have a handful of close friends you can go to when you need them. (This way you don't become a burden on any one of them, and it lessens the impact on you if one of them proves to be undependable.) Allow them to be ministers of healing in your life. You are the wounded one. You can "pay them back" when you're healthy again.

You might let your kids fill some of the needs in the home and in your heart but don't overburden them. Remember that they have been wounded, too. Other family members—your parents or siblings or even in-laws—can help with various practical needs. Try to keep a good attitude and a good self-image during this healing time. If you find that your family's efforts to help are actually hindering your healing process, find other avenues of support.

Restrain romantic and sexual needs for a while. You don't *need* to have a date for every social function, nor do you need to have sex. And either of these—sex or a compulsion for dating—can damage you in this time of healing. Get your life back together. Then you'll be in a position of regained strength and better able to make wise decisions.

One more word about need-meeting. As you sort through your needs and how to meet them, don't leave God out. God often uses the people around you to care for you, but other times He fills you with a sense of security, value, or purpose. God has a way of meeting needs when no one else can.

——— **MAKE IT YOUR OWN** ———

❶ What would you say are your five strongest needs right now? (Check five from the following list, or add your own.)

- ☐ Money
- ☐ Child care
- ☐ Self-esteem
- ☐ A sense of purpose
- ☐ A better place to live
- ☐ A way to make my kids listen to me
- ☐ Someone to talk to
- ☐ Courage to reach out to people
- ☐ A vacation

- [ ] People to do fun things with
- [ ] Sexual intimacy
- [ ] The feeling that I'm appealing to the opposite sex
- [ ] Forgiveness for my feelings of guilt
- [ ] To forgive someone else
- [ ] A hug
- [ ] Someone to care about my life
- [ ] A renewed spiritual life
- [ ] Other_____

❷ Now, in the spaces below, list the five needs you checked, and indicate *how it is being met* or *how it could be met*.

Need 1_____

_____

_____

Need 2_____

_____

_____

Need 3_____

_____

_____

Need 4_____

_____

_____

Need 5_____

_____

_____

❸ What could you do in the next week to ensure that your need-meeting network is working properly? To whom should you talk; what arrangements could you make? List what you need to do and when you'll do it.

_____

_____

_____

_____

> As a single parent, you are needy. Meeting those needs will involve some creativity, some reaching out for help, and a lot of hard work. The needier you are, the less you have to invest in a new relationship. Do not depend on a new romance to meet the needs of your life.

LEARNING TO DATE AGAIN

For at least a year after your breakup, you're in no position to date again seriously. For most people, recovery takes two years, and for some it takes longer. (Time this period from the "thud" of the marriage—when you were pretty sure it was over.)

So let's say it's been two years for you. You're rather well recovered (though still struggling with the practicalities of raising your kids alone), and suddenly someone asks you out. You think, "Hmmm. Yes, that *would* be nice." Where do you go from there?

At this point I'm talking about casual dating. But even casual dating involves risk. You put yourself on the line when you indicate your interest in someone. You lower your guard a bit as you agree to go out. Casual dating can be a healthy way of learning to trust the opposite sex again.

If you have already taken the time to re-establish your identity, your self-esteem, and your need-meeting network, you are in a good position to take the risk of dating.

———— MAKE IT YOUR OWN ————

❶ Which of the following are true of your "single-again" dating life?

☐ Nonexistent
☐ Casual
☐ Just some friends doing fun things
☐ Lots of dates with different people
☐ One special person has emerged
☐ I'm scared to death
☐ It's too much too soon
☐ Dating has helped to heal some old wounds
☐ Dating has re-opened some old wounds
☐ I have a hard time saying no to sexual intimacy
☐ I have a hard time trusting the opposite sex again
☐ It's really hard to meet good people to date
☐ My dates begin as good friendships
☐ My dates begin with a strong romantic spark

The best dating relationships arise out of friendships. And the best friendships are discovered within groups of like-minded people. So the first step to re-entry into the dating scene is to get involved with groups of people you like. For many, this is a church or church singles group. Or it could be a community group or special-interest group of some kind. Get out there and meet people.

———— MAKE IT YOUR OWN ————

❶ Which of the following might help you at this stage?

☐ Join a group of fun people
☐ Plan some group activities

☐ Get together for dinner with a group of friends every two weeks
☐ Enter a monastery or convent for some time alone
☐ Other?_____

Three years after his divorce, a friend of mine was invited to sing with the St. Louis Bach Society Chorale. He had been interested in classical music for a long time, though he hadn't sung it for twenty years. It was a great thing for him. He was with people again but in no hurry to find a new wife.

That's a healthy attitude for you to have. *Don't try too hard.* Build friendships with both sexes, free from romantic pressures. In this environment, healthy dating relationships can emerge.

You've probably known people who were trying too hard to find a spouse. It's as if they have a sign on their back that says, "Marry me!" They eat, sleep, breathe, *live* for that future relationship. But what happens? In many cases, potential mates flock to the ones who don't seem to care about getting married, the ones who are living their lives freely and fully on their own. What's going on here?

It's a matter of wholeness. The person who obviously needs marriage is essentially advertising a lack of wholeness. "I am not complete! I need somebody!" Prospective spouses are more interested in the one who *is* complete. That person would enter a relationship with more to offer.

——— **MAKE IT YOUR OWN** ———

❶ Which of the following might help you at this stage?
   ☐ Decide not to go on a serious date for another six months
   ☐ Find a good friend of the same sex
   ☐ Give yourself an affirming pep talk each day
   ☐ Take off that sign that says, "Marry me!"
   ☐ Other?_____

Beward of infatuation. Infatuation can be a nice feeling, but it can also hinder wholeness. What is infatuation? It is a celebration of your neediness. You think, *my life is worth nothing without this other person.* Can you see the problem? Infatuation does not help you become whole; it reduces you to nothing and gives someone else the power over your happiness.

When you are especially needy, you are very susceptible to infatuation. When you are already down on yourself, it is easy to worship someone who picks you up.

Infatuation may happen. You may find yourself smitten with someone. What do you do then? Go back to the basics: consider your identity, your self-esteem. You must march on toward wholeness.

If the infatuation goes beyond a passing crush, list your three best qualities and your three worst faults. Make the same list for the object of your affections. Look at those lists and remember: Both of you are on equal footing; you have good points and bad points. He or she will not solve all your problems, nor vice versa.

———— MAKE IT YOUR OWN ————

❶ Which of the following might help you at this stage?
- ☐ Write down the positives and negatives of both yourself and the object of your infatuation
- ☐ Develop a platonic friendship with this person
- ☐ Stay far away from this person
- ☐ Talk it through with a trusted friend
- ☐ Become famous so that this person will want you
- ☐ Other?_____

Have a mature attitude about looks. Our culture overemphasizes physical appearance. Look beneath the surface and find the human being inside. Find the ones who communicate with you soul to soul.

———— MAKE IT YOUR OWN ————

❶ Which of the following might help you at this stage?
- ☐ Stop watching TV for a week
- ☐ Evaluate your feelings toward the people in your life and determine how much is based on their looks

☐ Take time to find some inner treasure in someone you find externally attractive

☐ Hang out in a library and ogle the people with the highest IQs

☐ Other?_____

_____

Communicate with family and friends who are trying to help. Are your parents or siblings trying to fix you up with someone? What is your reaction when someone says, "Do I have someone for you"?

If you want certain friends to fix you up with people, tell them so. If you want them to stay out of your dating life, tell them that, too. If you feel they are pushing romance on you when you just want to find friends, tell them that. Those closest to you can help you or hurt you as you re-enter social life. Let them know how they can help.

────── MAKE IT YOUR OWN ──────

❶ Which of the following might help you at this stage?

☐ Tell your family and friends that they are *not* to try to fix you up with someone under *any* circumstances—never, no way, forget it! (Unless the person's really cute.)

☐ Tell your family and friends that you are interested in meeting new people, but that they should merely introduce you and then get lost.

☐ Tell your family and friends specifically about the kind of person you're looking for.

☐ Move.

☐ Other?_____

_____

Take slow, steady steps toward intimacy. When beginning the dating process again, take care to make wise decisions from the start. A bad experience at this point can be devastating and have a long-term impact. Look for your friends in the right places. Learning to trust again means taking slow, steady risks that are met with responsible responses.

I recommend this simple technique: Share-Check-Share. Share a little bit about yourself, then step back emotionally and see how the person responds before you share a little more.

FIG. 8.1

THE STAGES OF A RELATIONSHIP

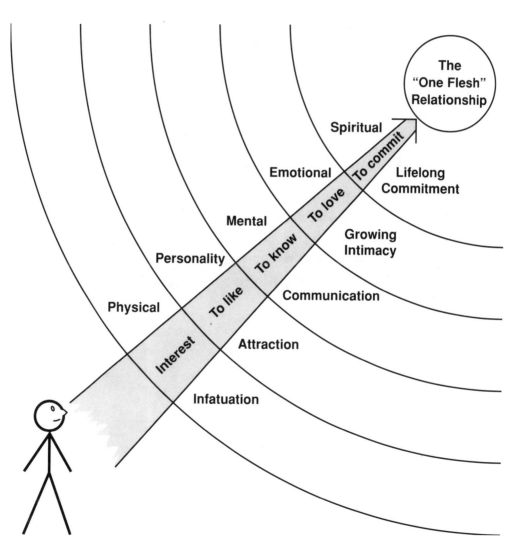

▶ Can he/she relate to what you are sharing?

▶ Can he/she share about himself/herself?

▶ Does he/she try to take advantage of your vulnerability?

Then repeat the same process again as the relationship grows.

As you can see in the diagram of the stages of relationships, your relationship needs to grow gradually through the stages of a committed loving relationship. Often in our society, people go from a physical attraction to sexual intimacy. Obviously, this is not God's intention for us. At some level we know that this behavior leaves us feeling more alone and empty. Proper intimacy grows slowly as we spend more time together and share at a deeper and deeper level. You are a complex creature that no one can fully know in a matter of months. Don't shortchange that process by settling for superficial intimacy.

——— MAKE IT YOUR OWN ———

❶ Which of the following might help you at this stage?

☐ Share more with the main person you're dating.

☐ Take time to "check" to make sure the other person can be trusted with what you're sharing.

☐ Slow down the relationship to make sure this intimacy is well-grounded.

☐ Play Scrabble together.

☐ Other?_____

_____

Move forward slowly in the re-entry process. Learn to be comfortable with yourself and do not look to other relationships to make you whole again.

MAKE IT YOUR OWN

❶ Of the major points presented in this section, which deserves most of your attention?

☐ Build dating relationships out of friendships

☐ Don't try too hard

☐ Beware of infatuation

☐ Have a mature attitude about looks

☐ Communicate with family and friends who are trying to help

☐ Take slow, steady steps toward intimacy

WHEN YOU'VE FOUND SOMEONE NEW

Don't expect to develop healthy relationships overnight. Go slow. This whole dating experience can be traumatic for you. You probably have a lot of baggage from the past to deal with—even some you're not aware of. If the person you're dating is not going to let you do that, then he or she will not prove to be a helpful long-term partner. Don't let someone pressure you into moving too quickly.

> Casual dating can be fun. Enjoy it. Keep it casual and friendly until you're ready for more. Regularly check your values. What do you want? What's important to you?

Go slow in terms in *frequency of dates* and the amount of time you spend together. It may be wonderful to spend time with this person. But you can be wooed into a fantasy world. Don't forget your responsibilities to your kids, to yourself, and to others. When you start spending every spare moment with that special someone, you may be getting too serious.

FROM DATING TO REMARRIAGE **203**

Go slow in terms of *amount of dependency*. In any relationship, you learn to depend on the other for certain things. Don't give up your hard-won self-sufficiency too quickly.

Go slow in terms of *sexual intimacy*. Outside of Christian circles, many assume that couples will be sleeping together by the third or fourth date. This is crazy and dangerous. It cheapens sex and it cheapens the people involved. Like it or not, sex carries a certain commitment. When you "bare yourself" to another like this, you are sharing a piece of your identity and welcoming another into your life. Outside of a marriage relationship, that physical intimacy is shallow, empty—a mockery of a sacred union.

Sexual intimacy is a slippery slope. One kiss wants another. The second kiss wants more. It is extremely difficult to dig in your heels and say, "All right, here's where I stop." But that's what you need to do. Make this decision *before* you hit the throes of passion and hold to it. This decision will allow your date to develop a genuine interest in you, not your sexual charms, and will keep sexual intimacy from propelling you into a bad relationship.

Go slow in terms of *involving your new friend with your children*. Your children will probably be curious about whom you're going out with, but you really don't need to introduce them to everyone you see casually.

When you start getting serious about someone, introduce them to your kids, and perhaps do some casual things together with your date and your kids. Go to a ball game or on a picnic or to see a good movie. Find out how your new friend interacts with your children and how they respond to him or her. However, you are not seeking another parent for your kids but a new companion for yourself. Give them all time to get used to one another.

As your new relationship grows, your children will ask you about it. Be honest, but don't divulge all the details of your dating life or your feelings about it.

Go slow.

MAKE IT YOUR OWN

If you are not yet beginning to date again, skip these questions. If you are, answer the ones that apply to your situation.

About how often do you go out on dates?_____

Have you begun to date one person exclusively or nearly exclusively?_____

How often do you go out with this person?_____

How often have you dated this person in the last month?_____

Do you feel this relationship may lead to marriage?_____

Why or why not?_____

_____

_____

Have you given up or neglected other relationships because of this new romance?_____

If so, which relationships?_____

_____

Has the frequency of your dates with this person been increasing?

_____

If you decided it was best to cut back on the frequency of your dates with this person by about 50%, could you do it? Would the other person understand?_____

_____

In what ways have you begun to depend on this person?_____

_____

_____

What things that your spouse used to do for you does this person now do?_____

_____

If this person had to go away for a month, how well would you cope?_____

In what ways does your new friend make you a better person?_____

_____

_____

Do you feel comfortable with your level of romantic/sexual intimacy with this person?_____

Have you talked about limits to your sexual intimacy?_____

_____

Which of you would be most likely to slow down or stop your sexual involvement?_____

Has this person met your children?_____

How much do your kids know about your relationship with this person?_____

_____

What do you think your children think of him or her?_____

_____

_____

Have your children asked you if you're going to marry this person?

_____

If so, how did you respond?_____

_____

_____

What, if anything, has this person done with you and your children in the last month?_____

_____

What does your new friend think of your children?_____

_____

Do you think your relationship would be better or worse if you didn't have children?_____

_____

Do you think your relationship *with your children* would be better or worse if you stopped seeing this person?_____

_____

In general, do you think this relationship needs to go slower, faster, or stay about the same pace?_____

Why?_____

_____

DATING WITH CHILDREN

For most of us, children add one more complication to an already difficult process. How should we involve our children, if at all, in our dating experience? The answer depends on the depth of the relationship and whether you are the custodial or noncustodial parent.

The Noncustodial Parent

In general, the noncustodial parent should use the time of designated visits to focus on their children. Introducing a new person, or even a series of female friends, can be counterproductive in building a close, trusting relationship with your children. Parenting needs to be your first priority when you are with your kids. Do your socializing when the children are not with you.

As one particular person becomes important in your life, then you may want to introduce him or her to your children in a gradual and nonthreatening way. Perhaps you could begin by inviting this person to be with you for *part* of the time the kids are visiting. But keep your focus on your children. If you are moving toward remarriage, you will need to involve your future spouse more and more, even if the children have some problems with this. Explain to the children where this new relationship is headed and how this will affect them. But don't jump the gun. To introduce your children to a progression of new love-interests in your life merely promotes instability in their relationship with you.

Never use a new relationship as a weapon against your ex, no matter how tempting this may be. And never use the children to deliver this blow.

The Custodial Parent

For the custodial parent, dating is difficult. Many date only on the weekends when the children are visiting the other parent. If that's possible, great. But don't be afraid to hire a baby-sitter and enjoy an evening out. You need to take time to rejuvenate yourself. That will make you a better parent.

A balance is required. If baby-sitters are seeing your kids more often than you are, that's a problem. You may need to limit your social life to one night out a week. Make sure that one night counts. Relax; find the emotional support you need. Don't think about the kids the whole night.

How will your children react? They may enjoy the fact that you're dating again. If they're very young, and if they like the baby-sitter, your night out can give them a "vacation" from you as well. There might be some initial fear of your departure, but once they realize that you can be trusted to come back, they should be better about this.

At somewhat older ages, your children may recognize the effect that dates have on you. If you are excited about going out, that can excite them, too. If you come home from a date happy and rejuvenated, they can share your joy. They are also aware of the imbalance of the single-parent family; they recognize that a remarriage could fill some gaps. In fact, in their minds they're probably running far ahead of you. One woman told me that her son met a man she was dating the third time they went out. The boy asked, "Are you going to marry my mother?" She was mortified. This is not an uncommon scene. Children are always putting the pieces together in their minds. And in the early stages of a dating relationship, the children may like the idea of a restored family unit. However, as you become serious in a relationship, your children worry. Not only is this new person competing with them for your love, he or she is also killing off their fantasy that mom and dad will eventually get back together. At this stage, children may lash out at you and become discipline problems. Assure them of your continuing love, but don't let them blackmail you. If you're developing a healthy new relationship, stay with it, despite their objections.

Teenagers often react with embarrassment. At this time, they are learning to deal with their own sexuality. The thought of mom or dad as sexual beings seems somehow inappropriate. Dating is something that kids do, not adults.

One woman told me of a church meeting that she and her teenage son were both attending—he with his teen buddies and she with her friends from the singles group. Before they left, he asked her, "Are you going to sit with one of the ladies or with Mr. Stokes?"

"Why?" she asked.

"Well, they're going to think that you're his girlfriend."

The fact was that she was just friends with Mr. Stokes, but her son was afraid of what his friends might think. He didn't want his friends thinking about his mom dating some guy. He was embarrassed about it.

In this stage, your children may belittle you and your dates. This can hurt, especially if your self-image is fragile. Be strong; weather the criticism. Remember that your teenagers' mockery stems from their own insecurity.

Be careful about how quickly you introduce your children to your dates. It is best not to introduce a person to your kids until the third or fourth date. And you probably shouldn't invite a date on activities with the children until you are dating that person exclusively.

Many single parents have the same trouble that teenagers do: Where can you find a place to be alone? If you both have kids, it may be very difficult to find those quiet moments together. If you're just talking, the problem's not as bad. Go for a walk, hit an all-night diner, or (if the kids are already in bed) sit in your living room. But if you plan to kiss and hug or display any similar intimacies, your options are more limited.

Good. You don't need to kiss and hug and all that other stuff. You need to talk. Use those physical limitations of space to impose physical limitations on the intimacy you share with your dates. Do not get sexually intimate with a date (even if you are observing certain limitations) at home when your children are there.

One of the greatest frustrations for single parents who are dating again is that the kids scare people away. Maybe it has happened to you. You meet someone at a party. Your eyes lock and you talk for hours. You have the same interests, similar temperaments. You find this person fascinating, and the feeling is obviously mutual. And then you let the cat out of the bag—

"As I was saying to my daughter just today..."

"Your daughter?"

"Oh, yes. Didn't I tell you? I have two. They're seven and five. Here, let me show you their pictures."

"How. . . nice. Hey, it's getting late. It was great talking with you."

Another one bites the dust. Children are instant responsibility. For many single people, this is a turnoff. It's painful for you to see this happen. It makes you wish sometimes that you didn't have kids. But it happens.

Here's the attitude you have to have. *That person, nice as he/she was, has a basic personality flaw—the inability to deal with the responsibility of having children. Therefore, he/she was not right for me.* It's not your problem. It's the other person's problem. You have children who are part of your life. They are a fundamental part of your personality. If someone accepts you, he or she must accept your kids. God may bring someone into your life who can do that—who can appreciate and accept that responsibility. Until then, you will continue to enjoy your children and the company of your friends.

You will be tempted to turn back the clock, to try to be the person you were B.C. (Before Children). But you can't, and it wouldn't be that great if you could.

——— **MAKE IT YOUR OWN** ———

❶ How have your children reacted to your dating?
- ☐ All for it
- ☐ It bothers them
- ☐ Embarrassed by it
- ☐ Eager for you to get married
- ☐ Compare your dating life to your ex's

Other?_____

_____

❷ How do you react to your children's reactions?
- ☐ It bothers me
- ☐ They heavily influence my decisions of whom to date
- ☐ They mildly influence my decisions of whom to date

☐ I feel pushed by them
☐ I'm frustrated because they're back and forth
☐ I'm doing my own thing, regardless of what they say
Other?_____

_____

❸ What "rules" have you set for yourself in terms of dating, especially as it affects your kids?_____

_____

_____

_____

❹ After reading this section, what rules *should* you set for yourself?

_____

_____

_____

❺ What reactions have you had from potential dates when they learned you had kids?_____

_____

❻ How did you feel about this?_____

_____

_____

Action Point: In the following space, write a memo to yourself, to your kids, or to God about your dating life. Include any resolutions you make as part of your Action Points, found in Appendix A.

MEMO

To:

From:

Re: My Dating Life

— 9 —

Remarried . . . with Children

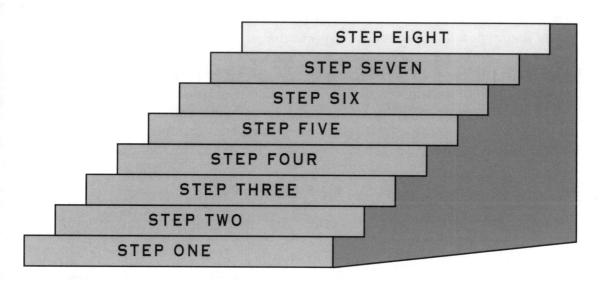

STEP EIGHT
STEP SEVEN
STEP SIX
STEP FIVE
STEP FOUR
STEP THREE
STEP TWO
STEP ONE

STEP EIGHT

Focus on learning how to unconditionally love others. Leave any possibility of a remarriage in God's hands.

Now your new relationship is getting interesting. You've been dating someone special for six months, maybe a year, and it feels good. You feel appreciated—finally. You feel that things are fitting together. You're beginning to think about the M word—*marriage.* And it scares you to death. After all, you blew it the first time. Marriage #1 ended in pain for everyone concerned. Why put yourself on the line again?

For many people, an anticipated remarriage causes agonizing ambivalence. Should I, or shouldn't I? Remarriage could really be good for me, or it could be another disaster. Am I ready to take that chance?

SPIRITUAL GROUND RULES

Before we delve into the emotional issues, let's examine the spiritual issues. In our society, most people don't think twice about the rights and wrongs of remarrying. It is assumed that if you struck out once, or even twice, you still deserve another time at bat. You may be assuming this yourself.

But many Christians (and some of other religious persuasions) believe that remarriage is wrong. They believe that the Bible teaches that divorce doesn't count in God's eyes, that a person is still morally bound to a spouse as long as he or she lives. Based on some of Jesus' teachings, they believe that any remarriage after a divorce is adultery.

I have many friends who believe this, and I respect their views. I especially respect their desire to follow the Bible's teaching even when it is difficult to do. However, I disagree with their interpretation of the biblical texts. I will not delve deeply into the arguments for and against remarriage (for that, see Jay Adams's book, *Marriage, Divorce and Remarriage in the Bible*, or Appendix C for an overview of the issues), but I want you to know my position. (If you are widowed or never married and feel free to remarry, you may want to skip to the next section.)

The Bible makes it clear that God hates divorce. God wants married people to stay married in warm, loving relationships. At the Fresh Start seminar, we do not encourage people to divorce. We urge reconciliation wherever possible.

However, human beings are sinful. We make mistakes. We hurt one another with the mistakes we make. In a perfect world, there would be no divorce. But this world is not perfect. And much of Scripture includes God's guidelines for making the best of a bad situation. God even set forth legal guidelines for divorce. He didn't favor it, but if it were done, he wanted to make sure it was done fairly. The Bible regularly urges special care for the victims of bad situations—the poor, the powerless, the widows, the orphans.

Within that context, I believe it is proper to treat most divorced people (of both sexes) as "widows." Their previous relationship has died. Their attempts to resuscitate it have failed. Just as a widow is free to remarry after a spouse's death, I believe it is legitimate for a victim of divorce to remarry—IF that divorce was based on biblical grounds and after the proper attempts to breathe new life into the old marriage have failed.

I am not talking about a situation in which someone says, "Oh, I'm tired of this spouse. I want to try another." That is still adultery, plain and simple, and it leaves many victims in its wake. Nor am I talking about a situation in which a couple says, "The old spark just isn't there anymore." Marriage is based on commitment. You need to keep your vows.

But once a biblical divorce has occurred, we still need to repent for the part we played in the breakup, pick up the pieces, and move on. Scripture speaks of God's mercies being "new every morning." If the old has died, we can enjoy new life. I know women whose husbands walked out on them eight, ten, twenty years ago. They have faithfully waited for their husbands to come back—even after the husbands have divorced them and remarried. They feel that they are still morally bound to the one they first married. I respect those women for their faithfulness, and I applaud their efforts to reconcile with their husbands and to keep trying until the last gram of hope is gone. But I believe that when the hope finally dies, Scripture allows us to pick up and move on, to create a new life for ourselves—perhaps with another spouse.

> From a scriptural perspective, remarriage is *not* the major issue but rather whether or not your divorce was biblical. The biblical grounds for divorce are (a) sexual immorality/adultery on the part of the spouse, and (b) abandonment by an unbelieving spouse. Christians are to offer forgiveness in both of these situations. But if a spouse does not repent, a divorce is legitimate. If you had a biblically grounded divorce, you have the right to remarry.

Where do I stand if my divorce was not biblically based? How does God view me?

Two basic principles apply:

▶ Do whatever you can to redeem the situation.

▶ Accept God's forgiveness and enjoy newness of life.

Study the Scriptures for yourself and consult with your church leaders to determine how these principles apply to your situation. See Appendix C.

———— MAKE IT YOUR OWN ————

❶ How would you define your beliefs about the rights and wrongs of remarriage?_____

_____

_____

_____

❷ If you are divorced, was your divorce on biblical grounds as we have defined them?_____

_____

_____

❸ What can you do to set things straight with God or with your ex-spouse?_____

_____

_____

Action Point: Do you still need to resolve issues from your former marriage? Do you need to

    ☐ Forgive your ex-spouse for wrongs done to you?

    ☐ Seek reconciliation with your ex-spouse, if possible?

    ☐ Confess your sins to God?

    ☐ Ask forgiveness from your ex-spouse?

In the space below, write a statement of resolution that does one of the four things listed above (if you have not resolved these yet). Address this statement to God, to your ex, or to yourself.

_____

_____

_____

_____

_____

When will you "deliver" this message?_____
Please write this statement and the target date in Appendix A.

THE RIGHT TO REMARRY

Just because you have the right to remarry, doesn't mean it's *right* for you to remarry. People remarry for many reasons, but some of them are not wise. Among these unwise reasons are these:

▶ "My children need a father."

▶ "We need financial security."

▶ "God meant for me to be married."

▶ "There's too much sexual pressure."

▶ "I'm so lonely."

▶ "I'm too busy to date around."

▶ "I need to settle down and start eating better."

All of these statements reflect real problems—but marriage is *not* the solution. Many of the problems you face will only intensify with a remarriage. And another difficult marriage will create more instability and emotional trauma for your children.

Consider remarriage with extreme caution. Even a "good" remarriage creates stress, and your kids may not deal well with it. Remarriage can raise questions of identity, create crises of loyalty, and foster confused discipline. If your single-parent family is in a weakened state, adding a new parent will not make everything better.

When the single-parent family has learned to cope, has regained a certain equilibrium, and has a sense of renewed strength—then a remarriage may be healthy. Even then, enter a new marriage with your eyes wide open, anticipating potential problems with the family, and not expecting a cure-all.

The right to remarry doesn't mean it's right for you to remarry.

LEARNING HOW TO COMMIT...AGAIN

Before considering remarriage, the last step you will take in dating is learning how to trust again, to commit again, to truly love again. For complete healing, we all need to reach a point where we can love others in a committed and unconditional way.

For many of us, this ability will be new, because we may not have had it in our first marriages. Unconditional love is actually impossible for humans to give on a regular basis, but it is what we constantly strive to achieve. It's the way God loves us. It is demonstrated in the fact that He loves us just as much on the worst day of our lives as when we are acting our best. His love is constant whether we are in the midst of an adulterous affair or sitting in church singing hymns.

Let me illustrate this point by telling you about my two weddings. At my first marriage, I was young, but I had all the answers. (Just like you at age twenty, right?) People would say to me, "Aren't you nervous? Are you sure you know what you're doing?" I would always answer with a confident, "Yes, I know exactly what I'm doing, and I'm not nervous at all."

I was telling the truth, I wasn't nervous, and I really thought I knew what I was doing, because I knew I was going to trust in God and He would always take care of me.

And when I said my marriage vows at my first wedding, I said with confidence that I would love my wife no matter what happened, and I would always be there for her no matter what the circumstances, and that I would put her needs before my own. Do you remember saying those things? Did we really have any idea what we were saying?

If you were like me, what you were thinking while you were saying those vows was more like, "Look at all I'm getting. A fine-looking wife, and she's going to help me get through school, and be there for me when I'm lonely, and..." My focus was on what I was getting, not what I was giving.

Now contrast that with my more recent remarriage. After being single again for about eight years and learning to be content as a single person, I was faced with the decision to recommit myself to another person, to trust again, and to love unconditionally. That was scary! As I thought about taking those vows, I now was thinking about the awesome responsibility I was about to take on.

I was going to promise to love, even when I was treated poorly; to communicate, even when I didn't feel like talking; and to put my wife's needs before my own. Can anyone do that on a regular basis?

I was nervous about getting married again, not because I loved my new wife less and not because I didn't trust her or didn't trust God. I was nervous because I knew I was setting myself up for a lot of hard work and failure—failure in the sense that I knew sometimes I would come home from a difficult day and my first thought would be, "Oh good. I'm home. Now I can relax and just do what I want to do." But inevitably, as I would walk in the door, my wife would say, "Oh good. I'm glad you're home. I need you to..." At that moment, would I be able and willing to love unconditionally?

It's a difficult task, but I believe that with God's help we can love others that way. Yes, we will fail, but that's where the work comes in. We must recommit ourselves constantly to the task of loving others.

———— MAKE IT YOUR OWN ————

We spend much of our lives in a struggle between being self-oriented and being love-oriented. The self-oriented person looks out for Number One. The love-oriented person considers the needs of the other person.

❶ When was the last time you chose to act in a self-oriented way rather than a love-oriented way? What did you do?_____

_____

_____

_____

_____

❷ What were the results? How did others respond?_____

_____

_____

_____

❸ When was the last time you chose a love-oriented response? What did you do?_____

_____

_____

_____

❹ What were the results/responses?_____

_____

_____

_____

❺ On a scale of 1 (self-oriented) to 10 (love-oriented), how would you rank yourself at the following times?

Weekday mornings just after waking up_____

At work_____

Just getting home from work_____

Just before bed_____

Saturdays at 10 A.M._____

Sunday morning at 11:30_____

❻ How do you explain the variation in these numbers? What factors are uniquely present in your "love" times or in your "self" times?_____

_____

_____

_____

_____

❼ What could you do this week to become more love-oriented? (Come up with three ideas.)

1._____

_____

2._____

_____

3._____

_____

Now jot one of these ideas in Appendix A, along with today's date.

OVERCOMING THE EMOTIONAL BAGGAGE

My friend Bob Hicks leads marriage retreats for churches throughout the country. He begins with a graphic illustration. He comes into the room loaded down with suitcases and bags. He works his way to the podium looking like someone who is going on a long trip. He has enough luggage for three or four people, and he appears quite disheveled. He then compares this comical scene to the way we all enter marriage. He says, "Sure you start off looking your best—in your best dress or nicest tuxedo. But the truth is, we all enter marriage looking more like *this* emotionally. We all enter marriage with a lot of baggage."

He then proceeds to open each of the bags to show their contents. One bag has a sign that reads, *Family of Origin.* Another says, *Previous Relationships.* It's a crucial point. This "baggage" affects every area of our lives together. And if we have been married before and have children, we'd have to add a *trunk* for each of our children and perhaps use a *dumptruck* to carry the baggage of our former spouse.

Hopefully, we scuttle some of this baggage during the dating process. While we deal with much of it in the early years of a marriage, some of it stays with us for the rest of our lives. If the baggage comes from our dysfunctional family background or a damaging previous relationship, then it is difficult to overcome the negative effects of these experiences.

Not all baggage is negative. Our children, our caution, and our commitment to make a better decision next time—this is all healthy baggage from our broken relationship. Most of us are much smarter today having learned from our experience.

The negative baggage usually far outweighs the positive. These remnants of the past get in the way of our new relationships, particularly if we remarry. For myself, I know that I deliberately took my time when I started a new relationship some eight years after my divorce. We dated for about three years as we both sought to heal from past wounds and former habits. Even after all that, after we were married, we still found baggage that was buried so deeply that it didn't come out until well into our marriage.

I was remarried for almost a year when my wife created a crisis in our relationship: She went shopping. Well I guess that wasn't the problem, since she had surely done that before without incident. This time, however, she came home late. She told me that she'd be home about dinnertime, which meant to me that she'd arrive around 5:00. Her dinnertime must have been different though, because 5:00 came and went and she hadn't come home yet.

I merely thought, "Oh well, I guess she's expecting me to fix dinner." So I started to whip something together quickly because I knew she'd be there shortly. Well, 5:30 came and went with dinner now on the table, but no wife. My emotions fluctuated between concern and anger as I waited from 5:30 until 6:00.

As my wife drove up a little after six, my mind was filled with questions. These came pouring out of me as she strolled in with her packages in tow:

"Where were you? Do you know what time it is? You could have been splattered in the streets somewhere. How was I to know where you were? Why didn't you call?"

My wife responded fairly calmly to my irrational inquisition. "It's only 6:00. I said I'd be home *around* dinnertime, and this is around dinnertime. Why are you so upset?"

As I continued to vent my frustration, my wife suddenly said, "Wait. I think there's someone else in the room with us."

Bewildered I looked around, knowing that we were home alone.

"What are you talking about?" I asked.

Astutely she responded, "I think your ex-wife is in the room with us. Your reaction tells me that there's more going on here than a general misunderstanding about the time I was expected home."

The words pierced my conscience. I knew immediately that she was right. Even though my former marriage had been over for some ten years, the incident brought back an unconscious memory that I thought had long been forgotten. There were times when my former wife went out, when I didn't know where she was, whom she was with, nor when she would be home. I suspected, and later knew, that she was being unfaithful to me. Those painful memories were part of the baggage I brought into my new relationship.

It's important, before a remarriage, to begin to identify our baggage from the past and to begin to talk through it with our intended. Other baggage may remain undiscovered until some event triggers our reaction. When it happens, perhaps we will be wise enough to recognize our unresolved issues.

As single parents, we all have baggage from the past that will affect our future relationships. It is important that we recognize this baggage and work through it in order to minimize its negative effects.

——— MAKE IT YOUR OWN ———

❶ What "baggage" do you carry in your attitudes toward

the opposite sex in general?_____

_____

a specific person of the opposite sex who shows an interest in you?_____

_____

your children?_____

_____

friends from when you were married?_____

_____

people at church?_____

_____

❷ How has this baggage created problems for you with

your children?_____

_____

someone you're dating?_____

_____

friends?_____

_____

❸ How can you get rid of this baggage?
- ☐ Talk it out with others
- ☐ Talk with your ex
- ☐ Talk with your children
- ☐ Talk to yourself
- ☐ Talk to God

In the space below, write a baggage-scuttling statement. You may need to pass this on verbally to someone else.

WHAT ABOUT THE CHILDREN?

A big part of our baggage is our children. If you are considering remarriage, you cannot ignore the needs of your children. For most of you, they have been your first concern. You must maintain an *objective* (if possible) and *balanced* concern for your children as you explore the possibilities of remarriage. *Objective,* because many single parents will rationalize remarriage as "best for my kids" because it's what he or she wants. *Balanced*, because you cannot ignore your own needs just because it might be difficult for your children.

I encourage couples to think through these issues before they become so close that they lose their objectivity. If you need to adjust your plans for the sake of your children, tell your intended well before making any serious plans.

The truth is, no matter what you'd like to believe or what your children might tell you, that a remarriage will be one more disruption in your kids' lives that will take them 2–5 years to adjust to. Blending families or adding one new parent to the formula is much harder than anticipated.

I teach a Sunday school class of remarried couples, and over thirty couples have attended from time to time. Each couple would be able to testify that their love, knowledge, faith, maturity, experience, and commitment were not enough to prepare them for the trials that a blended family would bring them. As we seek to support one another from week to week, I'm often struck with the thought that many would have postponed their plans had they known what they were going to have to take on.

A remarriage is not merely a continuation of an existing family with the addition of one new member. Rather, the remarriage constitutes a new beginning—one that drastically changes every "old family" interaction. Adding one new person to a family of three is not one new interaction but six new relationships—any one of which could be sour enough to cause turmoil in the whole family system.

The balance between your needs and your children's needs will vary from couple to couple. But for all of us, our first priority *before* marriage needs to be our children; *after* marriage our first priority is our new spouse. Therefore, realize why you and your children will view your marriage from opposing positions and feelings. While the adults are happy and riding high on their newfound love, the children are grieving the loss of their position, importance, and the fantasy that their parents "might get back together some day."

A mother single for thirteen years described to me how happy she was to be recently remarried, but she was confused by her son's reaction.

Before I married Jim, he and my son Paul were like best friends. I was so excited because I thought that now, after thirteen years of being by ourselves, Paul was going to have a father figure in the home. The strangest thing happened, though. As soon as we got back from the honeymoon, I noticed my son acting a little strange around Jim. Within a few weeks they were barely speaking, and now, after two years of marriage, Paul and Jim can't even look at each other without getting in a fight. I don't know what happened when Jim and I married, but something obviously clicked off for my son.

While this woman's story is hard to hear if you're considering blending your children into a new family system, it is certainly not unusual. And the more children you add, or if they are teenagers, you can certainly see how many things can go wrong! I paint this dismal picture not to scare you off, but so you will prayerfully and carefully plan before you make a decision toward remarriage.

If you are considering remarriage, complete the following section. If not, skip it.

❶ How would you rate the strength of your family right now?

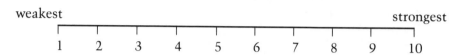

weakest   strongest
1   2   3   4   5   6   7   8   9   10

❷ How would you rate the strength of your family one year ago?

weakest   strongest
1   2   3   4   5   6   7   8   9   10

❸ If you marry again, how will your new spouse add to the strength of your family?_____

_____

_____

❹ How do you think your children will react to this new stepparent?

_____

_____

❺ Do you think that the children will resent the fact that they would have to share your love and attention with someone else?_____

❻ How will you as parents handle discipline in the "new" family?

_____

_____

❼ In what ways will the stepparent "replace" your ex?_____

_____

_____

_____

❽ In what ways will he or she *not* replace your ex?_____

_____

_____

_____

❾ Do your children want you to remarry?_____

Why or why not?_____

_____

❿ Do you think these are valid reasons?_____

Why or why not?_____

_____

_____

PREPARING YOUR CHILDREN FOR REMARRIAGE

If you're thinking about remarriage, read a book on the topic (see Appendix B). In the absence of such intensive help, consider the following guidelines.

Your Former Spouse Is Remarrying

One type of remarriage issue, not yet addressed, that affects you and your children, is the remarriage of your former spouse. You need to emotionally prepare yourself and your children for such an event.

▶ Deal with your own feelings. It is normal for you to have some feelings about the remarriage of your former spouse even though you thought you were completely over him/her. Many times this feeling is the jealousy of their "moving on with their lives" while you feel left behind. Deal with those feelings through a friend or a counselor. Do not let them taint your children's feelings toward their other parent or their new stepparent. Try to stay as neutral and emotionally uninvolved as you can in front of the children but encourage their discussion about how they view the pending changes.

▶ Encourage your children to participate in the wedding if invited. They may resist due to perceived loyalty to you, but you need to encourage them to take part in the ceremonies. Forbidding them will only hurt their relationship with *you* in the long run.

▶ Allow your children to talk about their new stepparent. Don't encourage their negative comments but empathize with their feelings, whether negative or positive. Try to remain emotionally neutral.

▶ Stay out of what goes on in the other household. You can't take everything your children tell you at face value. If the information seems particularly unusual, check out the story with your former partner at the next opportunity.

▶ Develop at least a casual relationship with the new stepparent. You need to be able to converse with him or her when arrangements are made for visitations, and you will certainly have to talk on the phone from time to time. Cooperation is a must if you want to help your children through this difficult time.

▶ Discuss with your former spouse the names to be used by the children when referring to their new stepparent. It is awkward for the children if you don't give them direction, and not discussing it can cause hurt feelings, especially *yours*. You might want to suggest to your former spouse that he or she discuss names with his or her intended and go over options with the children. Then, once all are in agreement, let you know of the decision so that you can reinforce it in your own home. Do not allow blatant disrespect for the stepparent, unless it is a case of temporary venting.

You Remarry

Your own remarriage may be a glorious time for you but may be a time of mourning for your children. Be sensitive to their feelings during this time and think about the following guidelines.

▶ Introduce the potential stepparent to your children in a gradual and nonthreatening way. In the beginning, fun outings are best, but these need to evolve into natural family times such as meals together, conversations, and even working in the yard together.

▶ Do not expect instant rapport between your children and the new stepparent. These relationships take time. In fact, some don't gel until a year or two into the marriage. (Some never do.) If things are going great, consider yourself blessed, but don't be surprised by strained relationships.

▶ Do not force your children to participate in your wedding. Invite them and explain that you would like for them to take part, but be sensitive to their loyalty to the other parent.

▶ Introduce the potential stepparent's children in the same gradual and natural manner the stepparent was brought into your family. Don't force relationships or expect friendships to develop. Work together on common projects or hobbies and see what develops naturally. Watch your natural tendency to favor your own children.

▶ Talk about the holidays and the customs and traditions that go with them in advance. You will probably need to blend traditions.

▶ Do not expect your children to ever love their new stepparent as much as their biological parent. (This is true for widows also.) This unrealistic expectation usually ends up hurting the new parent. Encourage your children to love and express love to their biological parent.

▶ Do not expect your children to call the new stepparent Mom or Dad. Usually some mutually agreed upon nickname is a better option and shows respect for the uniqueness of the other parent.

▶ Develop the respect of the children of blended families for the adults. From time to time the new stepparent will provide discipline. However, in the first few years, allow the natural parent to provide the primary discipline. For teens and some preteens, major conflicts can arise when the stepparent tries to exercise authority before he or she has earned any respect or credibility with the children.

▶ Avoid taking sides or disagreeing with your new spouse on discipline issues in front of the children. Present a united front for the children.

Discuss discipline issues privately, and then the natural parent should inform the children of your joint decision.

▶ Keep in mind that intense feelings of anger and resentment are normal in the blended family, especially among teenagers. Try not to personalize the anger and respond in a similar fashion.

▶ Be as patient and compassionate as you can, realizing that this transition is difficult for everyone. A transition can last from two to five years.

──── MAKE IT YOUR OWN ────

If you are presently dating and moving toward remarriage, then it is important that you work through this final Make It Your Own section. If you do not have a current prospect for remarriage, feel free to skip this part. However, come back to this section when you reach an appropriate point in your life.

Look at the guidelines immediately preceding this section. Put a check mark next to those guidelines that you think are potential issues for you and your prospective new family.

Then record those issues in the following space in order of importance. Make number one the most difficult issue you will face as a family; number two, the next most important, and so on. Try to come up with at least five issues you will need to work on. Feel free to list specific issues not already addressed.

1._____

_____

_____

2._____

_____

_____

3._____

_____

_____

4._____

_____

_____

5._____

_____

_____

6._____

_____

_____

(Use additional paper if you need more space.)

In counseling, I ask couples to identify the one issue whose resolution they feel is most critical before they can move forward in the relationship. Assuming your number 1 issue *is* your most critical area, write a goal and a strategy for resolving that issue for you and/or your children. Include a time frame in which you will try to resolve—or at least be working toward—the resolution of the problem.

Goal:_____

_____

_____

Strategies for Resolution:_____

_____

_____

Time Frame:_____

_____

_____

Action Point: Record your goal in Appendix A as one of your Action Points.

Once you resolve the most critical area, move on to the next, and then the next. On additional paper list the goals and strategies for each of the issues you identified. Some of these issues will be ongoing; they will never be resolved fully.

A FINAL THOUGHT

Your list of action points, issues, goals, and strategies will not guarantee an easy single-parenting experience or a good remarriage, even if you work through all of them. They can be tremendously helpful to you as you embark on this challenging life-style. I hope your time and effort will be richly rewarded as you try to be a contented, healthy, single parent, or as you try to successfully blend your family. Your children and *you* are certainly worth the investment.

Appendix A
Action Points

This appendix will contain a list of all of the action points or goals you have set as a result of this workbook. As you work through the material, record here any goals or commitments you make on behalf of yourself or your children. In this way, these pages will provide a quick review, as well as some accountability of the goals you have set. Refer to it often and proudly display the accomplishment of your goals.

GOALS   DATE ACCOMPLISHED

1. _____
   _____
   _____
   _____   _____

2. _____
   _____
   _____
   _____   _____

3. _____
   _____
   _____
   _____   _____

4. _____
   _____
   _____
   _____   _____

| GOALS | DATE ACCOMPLISHED |

5. _____
_____
_____
_____   _____

6. _____
_____
_____
_____   _____

7. _____
_____
_____
_____   _____

8. _____
_____
_____
_____   _____

9. _____
_____
_____
_____   _____

10. _____
_____
_____
_____   _____

11. _____
_____
_____
_____   _____

12. _____
_____

GOALS	DATE ACCOMPLISHED
_____	
_____	_____
13. _____	
_____	
_____	
_____	_____
14. _____	
_____	
_____	
_____	_____

Appendix B
Counseling References

The following books are recommended reading that deal with specific issues intended to supplement this workbook. If you have any trouble finding these books through your local bookstore, contact us at the Fresh Start offices. Call us at 1-800-882-2799.

Children of Divorce

Innocent Victims: How to Help Children Overcome the Trauma of Divorce, Thomas Whiteman, Nelson Publishing Co., 1993.

The Fresh Start Divorce Recovery Workbook, Burns & Whiteman, Nelson Publishing Co., 1992

Kids Hope: An Interactive Workbook for Children in Single-Parent Families (Grades 1-5), Gary Sprague with Randy Petersen, Singles Ministry Resources/Cook Communications, 1997.

Kids Hope: An Interactive Workbook for Teens in Single-Parent Families (Grades 6-12), Gary Sprague, Singles Ministry Resources/Cook Communications, 1997.

Parenting

Dare to Discipline, James Dobson, Tyndale House, 1970.

Helping Single Parents with Troubled Kids, Greg Cynaumon, Singles Ministry Resources/Cook Communications, 1993

The Key to Your Child's Heart, Gary Smalley, Nelson Publishing Co., 1988.

Parenting Alone, Ramona Warren, Cook Communications, 1993.

The Power of a Parent's Words, H. Norman Wright, Regal Publishing, 1991.

Raising Positive Kids in a Negative World, Zig Zigler, Nelson Publishing Co., 1985.

The Strong Willed Child, James Dobson, Tyndale House, 1978.

Ministry Leadership Tools

Building Your Leadership Team, Ed Weising and Wayne Fassett, Singles Ministry Resources/Cook Communications, 1995.

Creative Weekends: 23 1/2 Ready-To-Use Events for Your Single Adult Ministry, Paul Petersen, Singles Ministry Resources/Cook Communications, 1995.

Growing Your Single Adult Ministry, Jerry Jones, Singles Ministry Resources/Cook Communications, 1993.

The Idea Catalog For Single Adult Ministry, Jerry Jones, Singles Ministry Resources/Cook Communications, 1993.

One Kid At A Time: How Mentoring Can Transform Your Youth Ministry, Miles McPherson with Wayne Rice, Cook Communications, 1995.

Starting a Single Adult Ministry, Sue Nilson and Andy Morgan, Singles Ministry Resources/Cook Communications, 1994.

Relationships

Becoming Your Own Best Friend, Thomas Whiteman, Nelson Publishing, 1994

Love Gone Wrong, Tom Whiteman, Nelson Publishing, 1994

Sex and Love When You're Single Again, Tom Jones, Nelson Publishing Co., 1990.

Remarriage

How to Blend a Family, Carolyn Johnson, Zondervan Publishing Co., 1989.

Making Two Halves a Whole, Lonni Collins Pratt, Cook Communications, 1995

Self Image

Hide and Seek: How to Build Your Child's Self Image, James Dobson, Revell Publishing, 1971.

How to Really Love Your Child, Ross Campbell, Victor Books, 1982.

Telling Yourself the Truth, Backus & Chapian, Bethany Publishing, 1980.

You're Someone Special, Bruce Narramore, Zondervan, 1980.

Single Parent Family Ministry

Just Me & the Kids: Building Healthy Single Parent Families, Barbara Schiller, Singles Ministry Resources/Cook Communications, 1994.

Widows

The Grief Adjustment Handbook, Greeson, Hollingsworth, & Washburn, Questar Publishing, 1990.

The Widows Handbook, Foehner & Cozart, Fulcrum Inc., 1988.

Appendix C
Marriage and Divorce

Position Paper—Fresh Start Seminars, Inc.

I. WHAT THE BIBLE SAYS ABOUT MARRIAGE

A. Marriage is a DIVINE INSTITUTION.

Contrary to some contemporary opinion, marriage is not a human institution that has evolved over the millennia to meet the needs of society. If it were no more than that, then conceivably it could be discarded when it is deemed no longer to be meeting those needs. Rather marriage was God's idea, and human history begins with the Lord Himself presiding over the first wedding (see Genesis 2:18-25).

B. Marriage is to be regulated by DIVINE INSTRUCTIONS.

Since God made marriage, it stands to reason that it must be regulated by His commands. In marriage, both husband and wife stand beneath the authority of the Lord. "Unless the Lord builds the house, they labor in vain who build it" (Psalm 127:1).

C. Marriage is a DIVINE ILLUSTRATION.

In both Old and New Testaments, marriage is used as the supreme illustration of the love relationship that God established with His people. Israel is spoken of as the wife of God (see Isa. 54:5; Jer. 3:8; Hos. 2:19-20). The church is called the bride of Christ (Eph. 5:22-32). In Christian marriage the husband takes the part of the Lord Jesus, loving and leading his wife as Christ does the church; and the wife plays the role of the believer, loving and submitting to her husband as the

Christian does to the Lord. Thus Christian marriage should be an object lesson in which others can see something of the divine-human relationship reflected.

D. Marriage is a COVENANT.

From the earliest chapters of the Bible the idea of covenant is the framework by which our relationship to God is to be understood, and which also regulates the lives of God's people. A covenant is an agreement between two parties, based upon mutual promise and solemnly binding obligations. It is like a contract with the additional idea that it establishes personal relationships. God's covenant with Abraham and his descendants is summarized in the statement, I will be your God, and you shall be my people. Marriage is called a covenant (Mal. 2:14), the most intimate of all human covenants. The key ingredient in a covenant is faithfulness, being committed irreversibly to the fulfillment of the covenant obligations. The most important factor in the marriage covenant is not romance; it is faithfulness to the covenant vows, even if the romance flickers.

E. Marriage is a WHOLE-PERSON COMMITMENT.

God meant marriage to be the total commitment of a man and woman to each other. It is not two solo performances, but a duet. In marriage, two people give themselves unreservedly to each other (see Gen. 2:23-24; 1 Cor. 7:3-4).

F. "What God has joined together, let not man separate," declared our Lord (Matt. 19:6). "Till death do us part," is not a carryover from old-fashioned romanticism, but a sober reflection of God's intention regarding marriage (see Rom. 7:2-3; 1 Cor. 7:39).

II. WHAT THE BIBLE TEACHES ABOUT DIVORCE

A. Divorce is abhorrent to God (Mal. 2:15-16).

B. Divorce is always the result of sin.

God's basic intention for marriage never included divorce; but when sin entered human experience, God's intention was distorted and marred. Under perfect conditions there was no provision for divorce, but God allowed divorce to become a reality because of our sinfulness (see Deut. 24:1-4; Matt. 19:7-8). To say that divorce is always the result of sin is not to say, however, that all divorce is itself a sin. It may be the only way to deal with the sinfulness of the other party that has disrupted the marriage relationship.

C. There are two conditions under which divorce is biblically permissible.

Since divorce is a sinful distortion of God's intention for marriage, it is an alternative of last recourse, to be avoided whenever possible. However, Scripture does record two circumstances in which divorce is permitted (though never required):

1. In the case of sexual unfaithfulness (see Matt. 19:9).

2. In the case of desertion of a believing partner by an unbelieving spouse (see 1 Cor. 7:15-16).

D. Divorce carries with it consequences and complications.
Divorce, because it is a violation of God's plan, carries with it painful consequences and complications. God has made perfect provisions for the complete forgiveness of all our sin through the death of Christ, even the sins of sexual infidelity and unjustified divorce (see 1 Peter 2:24; Col. 2:13).

Forgiveness, however, does not remove the temporal consequences of our sins or the pain and grief involved in the death of a relationship. Divorced singles, single-parent families, remarriage, and the problems of "blended" families are part of the consequences of God's intention being thwarted. The church is to minister to individuals and families suffering these consequences and to seek to help them respond with maturity to their problems.

E. Reconciliation is preferred to divorce.
While divorce is permitted, it is never commanded. Forgiveness and reconciliation are always to be preferred (see 1 Cor. 7:10-11).

III. WHAT THE BIBLE TEACHES ABOUT REMARRIAGE

A. Remarriage is permitted, where the former spouse is deceased (see Rom. 7:2; 1 Cor. 7:39).

B. Where a divorce occurred prior to conversion, remarriage may be permitted.

"If anyone is in Christ, he is a new creation; old things have passed away; behold, all things have become new" (2 Cor. 5:17). When one becomes a Christian, all sin is forgiven; all condemnation removed (see Rom. 8:1). Thus, preconversion conditions do not necessarily preclude remarriage to a Christian mate.

If the former marriage partner has also become a Christian, remarriage to that partner should be sought.

Where the former partner has not been converted and attempts to share the gospel with him or her are rejected, however, remarriage to that person would be disobedient to Scripture (see 2 Cor. 6:14).

Even though remarriage is permissible biblically, there may be consequences from past sins that continue, or destructive patterns from the old life that can carry into new relationships. Thus a new marriage should be entered into with due thoughtfulness and with the counsel of mature Christians.

C. Where a divorce has occurred on scriptural grounds, the offended party is free to remarry.

A person who has been divorced because of infidelity of a marriage partner or desertion by an unbelieving partner, is free to remarry (see 1 Cor. 7:15).

D. What about desertion by a "Christian" spouse?

First Corinthians 7 deals specifically with the case of a nonbeliever who refuses to live with a believing spouse. The question then arises as to the remarriage of a believer who was divorced by a partner who also professed to be a Christian. Such a situation ideally should involve the church in the steps of disciplinary action outlined in Matthew 18. A Christian who decides to walk out of a marriage without biblical cause is in violation of Scripture. Such a person who refuses the counsel and admonition of the elders and persists in following the course of disobedience ultimately is to be dealt with as though he or she is an unbeliever (see Matt. 18:17). The deserted spouse would then be in a position of having been deserted by one whose sinful behavior and unresponsiveness to spiritual admonition gives evidence of an unregenerate heart, and thus falls under the provisions of 1 Corinthians 7:15.

E. Where a former spouse has remarried, remarriage is permitted for the other person.

Regardless of the reasons for the divorce itself, if one of the partners has remarried, the union is permanently broken and reconciliation is impossible, and thus the remaining partner is free to remarry.

F. Scripture does not absolutely forbid remarriage of a person who has caused a nonbiblical divorce.

Where there has been conversion (in the case of a person who was not a Christian when the divorce occurred) or the demonstration of genuine and heartfelt repentance (in the case of one who was a Christian at the time of the divorce), remarriage may be permitted for the offending party if (1) the former spouse has remarried or (2) the former partner refuses reconciliation (see 1 Cor. 7:15).

G. Scripture recognizes the possibility of separation that does not lead to divorce.

Because of humanity's sinful nature, couples can, at times, be involved in a marital relationship that is destructive, either physically or emotionally, to the two marriage partners and/or their children. It is possible that separation might become necessary because of the destructive nature of the relationship or the potential danger to one or more of the family members. Such a situation does not provide grounds for dissolution of the marriage and the establishment of a new marriage. Where no biblical ground for remarriage exists, a Christian is bound to seek reconciliation as long as there is a possibility of such reconciliation's taking place (see 1 Cor. 7:11).

IV. ANSWERS TO SOME RELATED QUESTIONS

A. Is there ever a totally innocent party in marital discord or divorce?

No one is ever free from sinful conduct or attitudes, so in this sense there is no "innocent party." However, some sins nullify the marriage covenant, and some, though they may be serious, do not. In any case of marital discord, both partners should be encouraged to try to understand how they personally contributed to the conflict.

B. Will divorced persons be allowed to participate in service opportunities in the church?

Spiritual, psychological, and relational maturity are primary qualifications for service opportunities. Divorce would be considered only one part of a much broader evaluation of a person's suitability for service. Divorce would not necessarily preclude serving. A primary consideration must be the reputation the individual has in the Body of Christ and the community (see 1 Tim. 3:2,7; Titus 1:6).

C. What if there has been no sexual unfaithfulness in a Christian marriage, but two Christians decide to dissolve their marriage because they are incompatible?

The Bible does not recognize incompatibility as grounds for divorce. Reconciliation must be achieved, and every means possible should be considered, including individual and/or marriage counseling. If Christ is on the throne of two human hearts, conflict will cease. He does not fight with Himself.

D. A frequent reason given for seeking a divorce is that the original marriage was a mistake. The couple believes that they got married for the wrong reasons and are asking why they should perpetuate a mistake.

God's promise is that He is able to cause all things to work together for good, even our human mistakes (see Rom. 8:28). The Bible does not recognize a "mistake" as grounds for divorce. A deliberate knowledgeable violation of God's revealed will for marriage is never an appropriate response to a mistake made earlier in life. "Two wrongs do not make a right."

E. What if a couple is separated or divorced, and both desire to have sexual intimacy with each other?

Sexual intimacy is the privilege of a marriage relationship. If the couple is already divorced, such intimacy would be classed as fornication. If the couple is not actually divorced, then sexual intimacy might be appropriate (see 1 Cor. 7:4-7). However, serious consideration should be given by both partners as to their personal motivation in the relationship. One of the considerations a couple must have is their reputation with their children and friends.